Langenscheidt's Universal Phrasebook

German

Edited by the
Langenscheidt Editorial Staff

D1576277

LANGENSCHEIDT

NEW YORK · BERLIN · MUNICH
VIENNA · ZURICH

Phonetic Transcriptions: The Glanze Intersound System
Illustrations: Helen Schiffer

Neither the presence nor the absence of a designation that
any entered word constitutes a trademark should be regarded as
affecting the legal status of any trademark.

© 1999 Langenscheidt KG, Berlin and Munich
Printed in Germany by Druckhaus Langenscheidt,
Berlin-Schöneberg

Here.	**Hier.** hēr.
There.	**Dort.** dôrt.
On/To the right.	**Rechts.** reshts.
On/To the left.	**Links.** lingks.
Straight on.	**Geradeaus.** gərädə·ous'.
Do you have …?	**Haben Sie …?** hä'bən zē … ?
I would like …	**Ich möchte …** ish mesh'tə …
How much does this cost?	**Was kostet das?** väs kôs'tət däs?
Could you please write that down for me?	**Bitte schreiben Sie mir das auf.** bit'ə shrī'bən zē mēr däs ouf.
Where is …?	**Wo ist …?** vō ist …?
Where *is/are* there …?	**Wo gibt es …?** vō gēpt es …?
Today.	**Heute.** hoi'tə.
Tomorrow.	**Morgen.** môr'gən.
I don't want to.	**Ich will nicht.** ish vil nisht.
I can't.	**Ich kann nicht.** ish kän nisht.
Just a minute, please.	**Einen Moment, bitte!** i'nən mōment', bit'ə!
Leave me alone!	**Lassen Sie mich in Ruhe!** läs'ən zē mish in rōō'ə!

Name	**Name**
Home address	**Heimatadresse**
Date of birth	**Geburtsdatum**
Vacation address	**Urlaubsadresse**
No. of *ID/passport*	**Nr. des *Personalausweises/Reisepasses***
In case of emergency please contact	**Im Notfall bitte benachrichtigen**
Important information (allergies, medicines, blood type etc.)	**Wichtige Hinweise (Allergien, Medikamente, Blutgruppe usw.)**
In case of loss of traveler's checks contact	
In case of loss of credit cards contact	

The Essentials
Personal Data

1 HUMAN RELATIONS

4 FOOD AND DRINK

5 SIGHTSEEING

6 SHOPPING

7 ENTERTAINMENT AND SPORTS

10 TIME AND WEATHER

241 GRAMMAR

HOW TO FIND IT

This phrasebook contains all of the most important phrases and words you will need on your travels. They have been divided up according to situations and organized into ten chapters. The chapter index at the page border will enable you to find things quickly.

Each chapter contains not only example sentences but also lists of words with complementary vocabulary. This will help you to form exactly the right sentence required for any given situation. The short, easy-to-understand grammar section will also help you.

For vital situations we have also included sentences that go from German to English so that a German speaker may also be able to communicate with you.

In order to cover as many different situations as possible we offer alternatives with many sentences; these are written in italics and separated by a slash, for example:

| *When/Where* shall we meet? | ***Wann/Wo* treffen wir uns?** |
| | *vän/vō* tref'ən vēr ōōns? |

You can transform the alternatives into individual sentences, asking either:

| When shall we meet? | **Wann treffen wir uns?** |
| | vän tref'ən vēr ōōns? |

or:

| Where shall we meet? | **Wo treffen wir uns?** |
| | vō tref'ən vēr ōōns? |

When more than two possibilities are given there is an ellipsis at that point in the sentence and possible completions are listed underneath, for example:

Could you please have this ...	**Können Sie das bitte ... lassen?** kẹn'ən zē dặs bit'ə ... läs'ən?

ironed?	**bügeln** bē'gəln
dry-cleaned?	**reinigen** rī'nigən
washed?	**waschen** väsh'ən

You can put them together as needed, for example:

Could you please have this ironed?	**Können Sie das bitte bügeln lassen?** kẹn'ən zē dặs bit'ə bē'gəln läs'ən?

You will also often find sentence completions in parentheses. It is entirely your choice whether to use them or not, for example:

What are the rates (approximately)?	**Wie viel kostet es (ungefähr)?** vē fēl kôs'tət es (ōōn'gəfär)?

We wish you a fun-filled stay in Germany and are sure that Langenscheidt's Universal Phrasebook German will be an indispensable companion on your travels.

HOW DO YOU PRONOUNCE IT?

All words and phrases are accompanied by simplified pronunciation. The sound symbols you find in *Langenscheidt's Universal Phrasebooks* are the symbols you are familiar with from your high-school or college dictionaries of the *English* language.

For German, these basic symbols are supplemented by seven symbols that have no equivalents in English. These seven are underlined – with the understanding that you may use the sound of the familiar symbol (the preceding symbol in the table below) until you have learned the specific German sound.

Symbol	Approximate Sound	Examples
	VOWELS	
ä	The **a** of **father**.	**Vater** fä'tər
ä̲	A sound that has to be learned by listening. (Pronounce the preceding vowel ä but much shorter.) *Until you have learned this sound, use the* **u** *of* up *or the* **o** *of* mother, *which will be understood.*	**Mann** män **ab** äp
ā̲	The **a** of **fate** (but without the "upglide").	**See** zā **Bär** bār

11

Symbol	Approximate Sound	Examples
ā	A sound that has to be learned by listening. *Until you have learned this sound, use the a of* fate, *which will be understood.*	**schön** shān
e	The **e** of **met**.	**Fett** fet **Äpfel** ep'fəl
ẹ	A sound that has to be learned by listening. *Until you have learned this sound, use the e of* met, *which will be understood.*	**öffnen** ẹf'nən
ē	The **e** of **he**.	**sie** zē
ē̲	A sound that has to be learned by listening. *Until you have learned this sound, use the e of* he, *which will be understood.*	**Mühle** mē̲'lə
i	The **i** of **fit**.	**bitte** bit'ə
ị	A sound that has to be learned by listening. *Until you have learned this sound, use the i of* fit, *which will be understood.*	**Müller** mịl'ər

Symbol	Approximate Sound	Examples
ī	The **i** of **time**.	**nein** nīn
ō	The **o** of **nose** (but without the "upglide").	**holen** hō'lən
ô	The **o** of **often**.	**wollen** vôl'ən **morgen** môr'gən
oi	The **oi** of **voice**.	**heute** hoi'tə
o͞o	The **u** of **rule**.	**Mut** mo͞ot
o͝o	The **u** of **book**.	**Mutter** mo͝ot'ər
ou	The **ou** of **house**.	**Raum** roum
ə	The neutral sound (unstressed): the **a** of **ago** or the **u** of **focus**.	**Mitte** mit'ə **genug** gəno͞ok'
N	This symbol does not stand for a sound but shows that the preceding vowel is nasal – is pronounced through nose and mouth at the same time. Nasal sounds have to be learned by listening. (Try not to use the **ng** of **sing** in their place.)	(in words of French origin:) **Orange** ôräN'zhə **Bonbon** bôNbôN' **Terrain** tereN'

Symbol	Approximate Sound	Examples

CONSONANTS

Symbol	Approximate Sound	Examples
b	The **b** of **boy**.	**bunt** bōōnt
d	The **d** of **do**.	**danke** däng'kə
f	The **f** of **fat**.	**fallen** fäl'ən **vier** fēr
g	The **g** of **go**.	**gehen** gā'ən
h	The **h** of **hot**.	**hier** hēr
ḫ	A sound that has to be learned by listening. This "guttural" sound resembles the **ch** of Scottish **loch**.	**suchen** zōō'ḫən **Bach** bäḫ
j	The **g** of **gem**.	**Dschungel** jōōng'əl
k	The **k** of **key**.	**kam** käm **Knie** knē
l	The **l** of **love** (not of **fall**).	**fallen** fäl'ən
m	The **m** of **me**.	**mit** mit
n	The **n** of **no**.	**nie** nē
ng	The **ng** of **sing**.	**Junge** yōōng'ə

Symbol	Approximate Sound	Examples
p	The **p** of **pin**.	**Plan** plän **gelb** gelp **Psalm** psälm
r	The **r** as spoken by most Germans has to be learned by listening. *Until you have learned this sound, use the r of run or fairy.*	**rufen** rōō'fən **viermal** fēr'mäl
s	The **s** of **sun** (not of **praise**).	**Glas** gläs **wissen** wis'ən
sh	The **sh** of **shine**.	**Schule** shōō'lə
<u>sh</u>	A sound that has to be learned listening. (It is somewhere between the **sh** of **shine** and the **h** of **huge**). *Until you have learned this sound, use the sh of shine, which will be understood.*	**Reich** rī<u>sh</u> **lächeln** le<u>sh</u>'əln
t	The **t** of **toy**.	**Tag** täk **Theater** tā·ä'tər
tsh	The **ch** of **much**.	**deutsch** doitsh

Symbol	Approximate Sound	Examples
ts	The **ts** of **its**.	**Zoll** tsôl **Platz** pläts
v	The **v** of English **vat**.	**November** nōvem'bər **Wasser** väs'ər
y	The **y** of **year**.	**ja** yä
z	The **z** of **zeal** or the **s** of **praise**.	**sind** zint **Eisen** ī'zən
zh	The **s** of **measure** or the **si** of **vision**.	**Jalousie** zhälōōzē' **Garage** gärä'zhə

Words of more than one syllable are given with a heavy stress mark (') and, in many cases, with one or several light stress marks (`): **Bremse** brem'zə, **Essenszeiten** es'əns·tsī'tən

A raised dot separates two neighboring vowel symbols (and occasionally two consonant symbols): **ansehen** än'zā·ən, **Ruine** rōō·ē'nə. This dot is merely a convenience to the eye; it does not indicate a break in pronunciation.

Human Relations

HI AND BYE!

Good morning.	**Guten Morgen!**	gōō'tən môr'gən!
Good afternoon.	**Guten Tag!**	gōō'tən täk!
Good evening.	**Guten Abend!**	gōō'tən ä'bənt!
Good night.	**Gute Nacht!**	gōō'tə näht!
Hi.	**Hallo!**	hälō'!

INFO Up till 10 am it is customary to say „Guten Morgen". For the rest of the day until evening „Guten Tag" is used, or „Grüß Gott" in Bavaria and Austria and „Grüezi" in Switzerland. In the evening, from about 7pm onwards, „Guten Abend" is used. The casual greeting „Hallo" is used at any time of the day especially among young people and colleagues. When leaving you say „Auf Wiedersehen" (polite form) or you can use „Tschüs", especially in Northern Germany and increasingly so in other parts of Germany, as a casual farewell greeting. When parting late in the evening „Gute Nacht" is used.

May I join you?	**Darf ich mich zu _Ihnen/dir_ setzen?**
	därf ish mish tsōō _ē'nən/dēr_ zet'sən?
How are you?	**Wie geht es _Ihnen/dir_?**
	vē gāt es _ē'nən/dēr_?

18

I'm fine, thank you. And you?	**Danke, gut. Und *Ihnen/dir?*** däng'kə, gōōt. ōōnt ē'*nən/dēr?*
I'm sorry, but I have to go now.	**Es tut mir leid, aber ich muss jetzt gehen.** es tōōt mēr līt, ä'bər i<u>sh</u> mōōs yetst gā'ən.
Good-bye!	**Auf Wiedersehen!** ouf vē'dərzān!
See you *soon/tomorrow!*	**Bis *bald/morgen!*** bis b<u>ä</u>lt/*môr'gən!*
Bye!	**Tschüs!** tshis!
Nice to have met you.	**Schön, *Sie/dich* kennen gelernt zu haben.** sh<u>ā</u>n, zē/di<u>sh</u> ken'ən gəlernt' tsōō hä'bən.
Have a safe trip home!	**Komm(t) gut nach Hause!** kôm(t) gōōt nä<u>h</u> hou'zə!

1

INFO In German there are two different forms of "you". The familiar form „du" is used to address children, friends and relatives in the singular, becoming „ihr" in the plural. The second form „Sie" (singular and plural) is used for all other adults and young people from the age of 14–15 upwards. When you get to know a person or a colleague better you can agree to use the familiar „du" form of address instead of „Sie". This is traditionally done by entwining your arms and drinking a sip of wine from your own glass. This creates a bond of familiarity and you can now call each other „du".

SMALL TALK ...

... *about yourself and others*

What's your name?	**Wie *heißen Sie/heißt du*?** vē hī'sən zē/hīst dōō?
My name is ...	**Ich heiße ...** i<u>sh</u> hī'sə ...
Where are you from?	**Woher *kommen Sie/kommst du*?** vōhār' kôm'ən zē/kômst dōō?
I'm from America.	**Ich komme aus Amerika.** i<u>sh</u> kôm'ə ous ämā'rēkä.
Are you married?	***Sind Sie/Bist du* verheiratet?** zint zē/bist dōō fərhī'rätət?
Do you have children?	***Haben Sie/Hast du* Kinder?** hä'bən zē/hä<u>s</u>t dōō kin'dər?
How old are they?	**Wie alt sind sie?** vē ält zint zē?
Do you have brothers or sisters?	***Haben Sie/Hast du* Geschwister?** hä'bən zē/hä<u>s</u>t dōō gəshvis'tər?

| I have a *sister/brother.* | **Ich habe *eine Schwester/einen Bruder*** |
| | ish hä'bə *i'nə shves'tər/i'nən brōō'dər.* |

| She'll be three. | **Sie wird drei.** zē virt drī. |

| What kind of work do you do? | **Was *machen Sie/machst du* beruflich?** |
| | väs *mäh'ən zē/mähst dōō* bərōōf'lish? |

| I'm a(n) ... | **Ich bin ...** ish bin ... |

| What are you studying? | **Was *studieren Sie/studierst du*?** |
| | väs *shtōōdē'rən zē/shtōōdērst' dōō*? |

... about home and vacation

| Is this your first time here? | ***Sind Sie/Bist du* zum ersten Mal hier?** |
| | zint zē/bist dōō tsōōm ers'tən mäl hēr? |

| No, I've been to Germany ... time(s) before. | **Nein, ich war schon ... mal in Deutschland.** nīn, ish vär shōn ... mäl in doitsh'länt. |

| How long have you been here? | **Wie lange *sind Sie/bist du* schon hier?** |
| | vē läng'ə zint zē/bist dōō shōn hēr? |

| For ... *days/weeks* now. | **Seit ... *Tagen/Wochen.*** zīt ... tä'gən/ vôh'ən. |

| How much longer will you be staying? | **Wie lange *sind Sie/bist du* noch hier?** |
| | vē läng'ə zint zē/bist dōō nôh hēr? |

I leave tomorrow.	**Ich fahre morgen wieder ab.** i<u>sh</u> fä'rə môr'gən vē'dər äp.
Another *week/two weeks*.	**Noch *eine Woche/zwei Wochen*.** nô<u>h</u> ī'nə vô<u>h</u>'ə/tsvī vô<u>h</u>'ən.
How do you like it here?	**Wie gefällt es *Ihnen/dir* hier?** vē gəfelt' es ē'nən/dēr hēr?
I like it fine.	**Es gefällt mir sehr gut.** es gəfelt' mēr zār gōōt.
Germany is a very beautiful country.	**Deutschland ist ein sehr schönes Land.** doitsh'länt ist in zār shä'nəs länt.
Have you ever been to the U.S.?	***Waren Sie/Warst du* schon einmal in den USA?** vä'rən zē/värst dōō shōn īn'mäl in dän ōō'-es-ä'?
You should visit me whenever you come to the U.S.?	**Besuchen Sie mich doch, wenn Sie mal nach den USA kommen.** bəzōō'<u>h</u>ən zē mi<u>sh</u> dô<u>h</u>, ven zē mäl nä<u>h</u> dän ōō'-es-ä' kôm'ən.
You're welcome to stay at my house.	***Sie können/Du kannst* gerne bei mir übernachten.** zē ken'ən/dōō känst ger'nə bī mēr ē̄bərnä<u>h</u>'tən.
I'd love to show you the city.	**Ich zeige *Ihnen/dir* gerne die Stadt.** i<u>sh</u> tsī'gə ē'nən/dēr ger'nə dē shtät.

SOCIALIZING

Would you like to ...?

Shall we meet *this evening/tomorrow*?	**Treffen wir uns *heute Abend/morgen*?** tref'en vēr ōōns *hoi'tə ä'bənt/môr'gən*?
Sure.	**Ja, gerne.** yä, ger'nə.
I'm afraid that won't be possible.	**Es geht leider nicht.** es gāt li'dər nisht.
I already have plans.	**Ich habe schon etwas vor.** ish hä'bə shōn et'väs fōr.
Would you like to join me for dinner this evening?	**Wollen wir heute Abend zusammen essen?** vôl'ən vēr hoi'tə ä'bənt tsōōzäm'ən es'ən?
I'd like to invite you to dinner.	**Ich möchte *Sie/dich* zum Essen einladen.** ish mesh'tə *zē/dish* tsōōm es'ən īn'läden.
When/Where shall we meet?	***Wann/Wo* treffen wir uns?** *vän/vō* tref'ən vēr ōōns?
Let's meet at ... o'clock.	**Treffen wir uns doch um ... Uhr.** tref'ən vēr ōōns dôh ōōm ... ōōr.
I'll pick you up at ... o'clock.	**Ich hole *Sie/dich* um ... Uhr ab.** ish hō'lə *zē/dish* ōōm ... ōōr äp.

I'll take you *home*/	**Ich bringe** *Sie/dich* **nach Hause**/
to the bus stop.	**zur Bushaltestelle.** ish bring'ə *zē/dish*
	näh hou'zə/tsōōr bōōs'hältəshtelə.

| May I see you again? | **Sehen wir uns noch einmal?** zā'ən vēr |
| | ōōns nôḫ īn'mäl? |

No, thanks!

| I already have plans. | **Ich habe schon was vor.** ish hä'bə |
| | shōn väs fôr. |

| I'm waiting for | **Ich warte auf jemanden.** ish vär'tə |
| someone. | ouf yā'mändən. |

| Please leave me alone! | **Lassen Sie mich bitte in Ruhe!** läs'ən |
| | zē mish in rōō'ə! |

| Go away! | **Verschwinde!** fərshvin'də! |

COMMUNICATING

| Does anyone here | **Spricht hier jemand Englisch?** |
| speak English? | shprisht hēr yā'mänt eng'lish? |

| **?** **Sprechen Sie Deutsch?** | Do you speak |
| • shpresh'ən zē doitsh? | German? |

| Only a little. | **Nur wenig.** nōōr vā'nish. |

24

Please speak a little slower.	**Bitte sprechen Sie etwas langsamer.** bit'ə shpresh'ən zē et'vās läng'zämər.
Do you understand?	***Haben Sie/Hast du verstanden?*** *hä'bən zē/häst dōō fərshtän'dən?*
I understand.	**Ich habe verstanden.** ish hä'bə fərshtän'dən.
I didn't understand that.	**Ich habe das nicht verstanden.** ish hä'bə däs nisht fərshtän'dən.
Please repeat that.	**Sagen Sie es bitte noch einmal.** zä'gən zē es bit'ə nōh in'mäl.
What is this called in German?	**Wie heißt das auf Deutsch?** vē hist däs ouf doitsh?
What does … mean?	**Was bedeutet …?** väs bədoi'tət …?
Please write it down for me.	**Schreiben Sie es mir bitte auf.** shri'bən zē es mēr bit'ə ouf.

WHAT DO YOU THINK?

It *was/is* very nice here.	**Es *war/ist* sehr schön hier.** es wär/ist zār shän hēr.
I'm very satisfied.	**Ich bin sehr zufrieden!** ish bin zār tsōōfrē'dən!

1

Great!	**Prima!** prē'mä!
I like it.	**Es gefällt mir.** es gəfelt' mēr.
Good idea.	**Eine gute Idee.** ī'nə gōō'tə idā'.
OK.	**In Ordnung.** in ôrd'nōōng.
It's all the same to me.	**Das ist mir egal.** däs ist mēr āgäl'.
I don't know yet.	**Ich weiß noch nicht.** ish vīs nôh nisht.
Perhaps.	**Vielleicht.** fēlīsht'.
Probably.	**Wahrscheinlich.** värshīn'lish.
That's very annoying.	**Das ist sehr ärgerlich.** däs ist zār er'gərlish.
Too bad!	**Wie schade!** vē shä'də!
Unfortunately that's impossible.	**Das geht leider nicht.** däs gāt lī'dər nisht.
I don't like it.	**Das gefällt mir nicht.** däs gəfelt' mēr nisht.
I would rather not.	**Das möchte ich lieber nicht.** däs mesh'tə ish lē'bər nisht.
Absolutely not.	**Auf keinen Fall.** ouf kī'nən fäl.

BASIC PHRASES

Please; Thank you

Could you please help me?	**Können Sie mir bitte helfen?** ken'tən zē mēr bi'tə hel'fən?
No, thank you.	**Nein, danke.** nīn, däng'kə.
Yes, please.	**Ja, bitte.** yä, bit'ə.
Thank you, same to you.	**Danke, gleichfalls.** däng'kə, glīsh'fäls.
Thank you, that's very nice of you.	**Vielen Dank, das ist sehr nett von Ihnen.** vē'lən dängk, däs ist zār net fôn ē'nən.
Thank you very much for your *effort/help*.	**Vielen Dank für Ihre *Mühe/Hilfe*.** vē'lən dängk fēr ē'rə *mē'ə/hil'fə*.
You're welcome.	**Bitte sehr.** bit'ə zār.
My pleasure.	**Gern geschehen.** gern gəshā'ən.
May I?	**Darf ich?** därf ish?

I'm sorry!

| Excuse me. | **Entschuldigung.** entshool'digoong. |
| That's OK. | **Bitte.** bit'ə. |

I'm sorry about that.	**Das tut mir Leid.** däs tōōt mēr līt.
That's OK.	**Das macht nichts.** däs mäht nishts.
That upsets me.	**Das ist mir peinlich.** däs ist mēr pīn'lish.
It was a misunderstanding.	**Das war ein Missverständnis.** däs vär īn mis'fərstend'nis.

Best wishes!

Congratulations!	**Herzlichen Glückwunsch!** herts'-lishən glik'vōōnsh!
Happy birthday!	**Herzlichen Glückwunsch (zum Geburtstag)!** herts'lishən glik'vōōnsh (tsōōm gəbōōrts'täk)!
Get well soon!	**Gute Besserung!** gōō'tə bes'ərōōng!
Have a good trip!	**Gute Reise!** gōō'tə rī'zə!
Enjoy *yourself/ yourselves!*	**Viel Spaß!** fēl shpäs!
Merry Christmas!	**Frohe Weihnachten!** frō'ə vī'nähtən!
Happy New Year!	**Frohes Neues Jahr!** frō'əs noi'əs yär!
Happy Easter!	**Frohe Ostern!** frō'ə ōs'tərn!

address	**die Adresse**	dē ădres'ə
alone	**allein**	ălīn'
to arrive	**ankommen**	än'kômən
brother	**der Bruder**	dār brōō'dər
child	**das Kind**	däs kint
city	**die Stadt**	dē shtät
to come from	**kommen aus**	kôm'ən ous
country	**das Land**	däs länt
daughter	**die Tochter**	dē tôḫ'tər
father	**der Vater**	dār fä'tər
fiancé	**der Verlobte**	dār fərlōp'tə
fiancée	**die Verlobte**	dē fərlōp'tə
free	**frei**	frī
friend	**der Freund; die Freundin**	dār froint, dē froin'din
to get to know	**kennen lernen**	ken'ən ler'nən
girlfriend	**die Freundin**	dē froin'din
to go dancing	**tanzen gehen**	tän'tsen gē'ən
to go out to eat	**essen gehen**	es'ən gā'ən
to have plans	**etwas vorhaben**	et'wäs fōr'häbən
husband	**der Mann**	dār män
to invite (*someone*) to dinner	**zum Essen einladen**	tsōōm es'ən īn'lädən
job	**der Beruf**	dār bərōōf'

to know	**wissen** vis'ən
to leave	**abfahren** äp'färən
to like	**mögen** mȫ'gən
I like it	**es gefällt mir** es gəfelt' mēr
little	**wenig** vā'nish
to make a date	**sich verabreden** zish fəräp'rādən
married	**verheiratet** fərhī'rätət
to meet with	**sich treffen mit** zish tref'ən mit
mother	**die Mutter** dē mŏŏt'ər
my name is	**ich heiße** ish hī'sə
occupied	**besetzt** bəzetst'
old	**alt** ält
perhaps	**vielleicht** fēlīsht'
photograph	**das Foto** däs fō'tō
please	**bitte** bit'ə
to repeat	**wiederholen** vēdərhō'lən
to return	**wiederkommen** vē'dərkômən
satisfied	**zufrieden** tsōōfrē'dən
school	**die Schule** dē shōō'lə
to see … again	**wiedersehen** vē'dərzā'ən
siblings	**die Geschwister** *(plural)* dē gəshvis'tər
sister	**die Schwester** dē shves'tər
son	**der Sohn** där zōn
to speak	**sprechen** shpresh'ən
student	**der Student; die Studentin** där shtōōdent'; dē shtōōden'tin

to stay overnight	**übernachten** ēbərnäh'tən
to study	**studieren** shtōōdē'rən
to take (*someone*) home	**nach Hause bringen** näh hou'zə bring'ən
thank you	**danke** däng'kə
to understand	**verstehen** fərshtā'ən
vacation	**der Urlaub** där ōōr'loup
to wait	**warten** vär'tən
wife	**die Frau** dē frou
to write down	**aufschreiben** ouf'shrībən

FOR THE HANDICAPPED

| I'm hard of hearing. Can you speak a little louder? | **Ich höre schlecht. Können Sie ein bisschen lauter sprechen?** ish hā'rə shlesht. ken'ən zē īn bis'shən lou'tər shpresh'ən? |

| Can you please write that down? | **Können Sie das bitte aufschreiben?** ken'ən zē däs bit'ə ouf'shrībən? |

| I'm physically handicapped. Can you please help me? | **Ich bin körperbehindert. Können Sie mir bitte helfen?** ish bin kār'pərbəhin'dərt. ken'ən zē mēr bit'ə hel'fən? |

Take hold here.	**Fassen Sie bitte hier an.** fäs'ən zē bit'ə hēr än.
Do you have a wheelchair for me?	**Haben Sie einen Rollstuhl für mich?** hä'bən zē i'nən rol'shtōōl fēr mish?
Can you please take my luggage to the *room/taxi*?	**Können Sie mir bitte das Gepäck *aufs Zimmer/zum Taxi* tragen?** ken'ən zē mēr bit'ə däs gəpek' *oufs tsim'ər/tsōōm täk'sē* trä'gən?
Where is the nearest elevator?	**Wo ist der nächste Fahrstuhl?** vō ist där nā<u>sh</u>'stə fär'shtōōl?
Could you please dial for me? The telephone is too high up.	**Können Sie bitte für mich wählen? Das Telefon hängt zu hoch.** ken'ən zē bit'ə fēr mish vā'lən? däs tālāfōn' hengt tsōō hō<u>h</u>.
Is it suitable for wheelchairs?	**Ist es für Rollstuhlfahrer geeignet?** ist es fēr rol'shtōōlfä'rər gə-īg'nət?
Is there a ramp there for wheelchairs?	**Gibt es dort eine Rampe für Rollstuhlfahrer?** gēpt es dôrt i'nə räm'pə fēr rol'shtōōlfä'rər?
Where is the rest room for the handicapped?	**Wo ist hier eine Behindertentoilette?** vō ist hēr i'nə bəhin'dərtəntô-älet'ə?

| I need someone to accompany me. | **Ich brauche jemanden, der mich begleitet.** ish brou'ḥə yā'mändən, dār mish bəgli'tət. |

| Do you have a seat where I can stretch my legs out? | **Haben Sie einen Platz, wo ich meine Beine ausstrecken kann?** hä'bən zē i'nən pläts, vō ish mī'nə bī'nə ous'shtrekən kän? |

BUSINESS CONTACTS

On the Phone

| This is … of … | **Hier ist … von der Firma …** hēr ist … fôn dār fir'mä … |

| I would like to speak to … | **Ich möchte … sprechen.** ish mesh'tə …shpresh'ən. |

❗ Ich verbinde. ish fərbin'də. — I'll connect you.

❗ … spricht gerade. … shprisht gərä'də. — … is busy at the moment.

❗ … ist heute nicht im Haus. … ist hoi'tə nisht im hous. — … is not here today.

❓ Möchten Sie eine Nachricht hinterlassen? mesh'tən zē i'nə näḥ'risht hintərläs'ən? — Would you like to leave a message?

May I leave a message for …?	**Kann ich eine Nachricht für … hinterlassen?** kän i<u>sh</u> ī'nə nä<u>h</u>'ri<u>sh</u>t fēr … hintərläs'ən?	

At the Reception Desk

I need to see …	**Ich möchte zu …** i<u>sh</u> me<u>sh</u>'tə tsoo …	
My name is …	**Mein Name ist …** mīn nä'mə ist …	
I have an appointment at … o'clock with …	**Ich habe um … Uhr einen Termin mit …** i<u>sh</u> hä'bə oom … oor ī'nən termēn' mit …	

Einen Moment, bitte. ī'nən mōment', bit'ə.	One moment, please.
Würden Sie sich bitte hier eintragen? vir'dən zē zi<u>sh</u> bit'ə hēr in'trägən?	Would you please register here?
… kommt sofort. … kômt zōfôrt'.	… will be right here.
… ist noch in einer Besprechung. … ist nô<u>h</u> in ī'nər bəshpre<u>sh</u>'oong.	… is still in a meeting.
Kommen Sie bitte mit mir. Ich bringe Sie zu … kôm'ən zē bit'ə mit mēr. i<u>sh</u> bring'ə zē tsoo …	Please follow me. I'll show you to …

? **Würden Sie bitte hier einen Moment warten?** vir'dən zē bit'ə hēr i'nən mōment' vär'tən?

Would you please wait here a moment?

? **Darf ich Ihnen einen Kaffee bringen?** därf ish ē'nən i'nən käf'ā bring'ən?

May I serve you some coffee?

At Trade Fairs

I'm looking for the ... booth.

Ich suche den Stand der Firma ... ish zōō'hə dän shtänt där fir'mä ...

! **Halle ..., Stand ...** häl'ə ..., shtänt ...

Hall ..., booth ...

Do you have any brochures on ...?

Haben Sie Informationsmaterial über ...? hä'bən zē infôrmätsyöns'-mätərē·äl' ē'bər ...?

Do you also have pamphlets in English?

Haben Sie auch Prospekte auf Englisch? hä'bən zē ouh prōspek'tə ouf eng'lish?

Who can I ask?

An wen kann ich mich wenden? än vān kän ish mish ven'dən?

Who is your agent in the U.S.?

Wer ist Ihr Agent in den USA? vār ist ēr ägent' in dän ōō'-es-ä'?

1

35

Here is my card.	**Hier ist meine Karte.** hēr ist mi'nə kär'tə.

Business Contacts

administration	**das Verwaltungsgebäude** däs fərväl'tōōngsgəboi'də
building	
agent	**der Agent** där ägent'
appointment	**der Termin** där termēn'
booth	**der Stand** där shtänt
boss	**der Chef** där shef
brochures	**das Informationsmaterial** däs infôrmätsyōns'mäterē-äl'
building	**das Gebäude** däs gəboi'də
business card	**die Visitenkarte** dē vēzēt'ənkärtə
cabin	**die Kabine** dē käbē'nə
catalog	**der Katalog** där kätälōk'
concern	**der Konzern** där kôntsern'
conference	**die Konferenz** dē kônfərents'
conference room	**der Besprechungsraum** där bəshpre<u>sh</u>'ōōngsroum`
contact	**der Ansprechpartner** där än'shpre<u>sh</u>pärt`nər
copy	**die Kopie** dē kôpē'
customer	**der Kunde** där kōōn'də
department	**die Abteilung** dē äpti'lōōng

department head	**der Abteilungsleiter** dār äpti'lо̄о̄ngslī'tər	
documents	**die Unterlagen** *(plural)* dē о̄о̄n'tərlägən	
entrance	**der Eingang** dār īn'gäng	
exit	**derAusgang** dār ous'gäng	
fair	**die Messe** dē mes'ə	
fax machine	**das Telefax** däs tā' läfäks	
floor	**die Etage** dē etä'zhə	
general agency	**die Generalvertretung** dē genərāl'fərtrātо̄о̄ng	
information booth	**der Informationsstand** dār infôrmätsyо̄ns'shtänt	
license	**die Lizenz** dē lïtsens'	
manager	**der Geschäftsführer** dār gəshefts'fēr̄ər	
marker	**der Filzstift** dār fïlts'shtïft	
marketing	**der Vertrieb** dār fərtrēp'	
to meet	**sich treffen** zish tref'ən	
meeting	**die Besprechung** dē bəshpresh'о̄о̄ng	
meeting	**das Treffen** däs tref'ən	
news	**die Nachricht** dē näh'rïsht	
to notify	**benachrichtigen** bənäh'rïshtigən	
office	**das Büro** däs bērо̄'	
to phone	**telefonieren** tālāfо̄nē'rən	
price	**der Preis** dār prïs	
price list	**die Preisliste** dē prïs'listə	

prospectus	**der Prospekt** där prŏspekt'
reception	**der Empfang** där empfäng'
representative	**der Vertreter** där fərträ'tər
sample	**das Muster** däs mōōs'tər
secretary	**die Sekretärin** dē sekretä'rin
secretary's office	**das Sekretariat** däs sek`rətärē-ät'
session	**die Sitzung** dē zits'ōōng
subsidiary	**die Tochtergesellschaft** dē tôḫ'tərgəzel`shäft
telephone	**das Telefon** däs täläfōn'

Accommodations

INFORMATION

Do you know where I can find a room here?	**Wissen Sie, wo ich hier ein Zimmer finden kann?** vĭs'ən zē, vō i͟sh hēr ĭn tsĭm'ər fĭn'dən kän?
Could you recommend a *reasonably-priced hotel/motel?*	**Können Sie mir *ein preiswertes Hotel/ein Motel* empfehlen?** kĕn'ən zē mēr ĭn prīs'vertəs hōtel´/ĭn mōtel´ empfā'lən?
I'm looking for somewhere to stay ...	**Ich suche eine Unterkunft ...** i͟sh zōō'hə i'nə ōōn'tərkōōnft ...
in a *central/quiet* location.	**in *zentraler/ruhiger* Lage.** ĭn tsenträ'lər/rōō'igər lä'gə.
at the beach.	**am Strand.** äm shtränt.
by the river.	**am Fluss.** äm flōōs.
What are the rates (approximately)?	**Wie viel kostet es (ungefähr)?** vē fēl kôs'tət es (ōōn'gəfär)?
Can you make a reservation for me there?	**Können Sie dort für mich reservieren?** kĕn'ən zē dôrt fēr mi͟sh räzervē'rən?
Is there a camping ground here?	**Gibt es hier einen Campingplatz?** gēpt es hēr i'nən kem'pĭngpläts´?
Is it far from here?	**Ist es weit von hier?** ĭst es vīt fôn hēr?

| How do I get there? | **Wie komme ich dorthin?** |
| | vē kôm'ə ish dôrt·hin'? |

| Can you draw me a map? | **Können Sie mir den Weg aufzeichnen?** |
| | ken'ən zē mēr dän vāk ouf'tsīshnən? |

HOTEL AND VACATION RENTAL

Hotel

| I have a reservation. My name is … | **Für mich ist bei Ihnen ein Zimmer reserviert. Mein Name ist …** fēr mish |
| | ist bī ē'nən in tsim'ər rāzervērt'. min nä'mə ist … |

| Here is my confirmation (number). | **Hier ist meine Bestätigung.** |
| | hēr ist mī'nə bəshtā'tigōōng. |

| Do you have a *double/single* room available … | **Haben Sie ein *Doppelzimmer/Einzel-zimmer* frei …** hä'bən zē in |
| | *dôp'əltsim'ər/īn'tseltsim'ər* frī … |

for *one night/ … nights*?	**für *einen Tag/…Tage*?**
	fēr *ī'nən täk/…tä'gə*?
with a balcony?	**mit Balkon?** mit bälkông'?
with a view of the ocean?	**mit Blick aufs Meer?**
	mit blik oufs mār?

41

toward the	**nach _hinten/vorne_ heraus?**
back/front?	näh _hin'tən/fôr'nə_ herous'?
with air conditioning?	**mit Klimaanlage?**
	mit klē'mä·än'lägə?

! **Wir sind leider ausgebucht.** Unfortunately, we are
● vēr zint lī'dər ous'gəbōōḫt. fully booked.

Tomorrow/On the ...	_Morgen/Am ..._ **wird ein Zimmer frei.**
there will be a room	_môr'gən/äm_ ... virt īn tsim'ər frī.
available.	

| What is the rate _with/_ | **Wie viel kostet es _mit/ohne_ Frühstück?** |
| _without_ breakfast? | vē fēl kôs'tət es _mit/ō'nə_ frē'shtĭk? |

INFO The price for breakfast is usually included in hotel
charges. In almost all hotels these days this means
a generous breakfast buffet. However, in private accommodations
and lodging houses you are likely to be offered the much simpler
continental breakfast of tea or coffee, rolls with butter and jam,
and perhaps some cold sliced meat or cheese. If you want an egg
you will probably have to pay extra.

| Is there a discount | **Gibt es eine Ermäßigung für Kinder?** |
| for children? | gēpt es ī'nə ermä'sigōōng fēr kin'dər? |

42

Is there a discount if I stay … nights?	**Gibt es eine Ermäßigung, wenn man … Tage bleibt?** gēpt es i'nə ermā'sigōōng, ven mān … tä'gə blīpt?
Can I pay by credit card?	**Kann ich mit Kreditkarte bezahlen?** kän ish mit krādit'kärtə bətsä'lən?
May I have a look at the room?	**Kann ich mir das Zimmer ansehen?** kän ish mēr däs tsim'ər än'zā·ən?
Can you set up *an additional bed/a crib* in the room?	**Können Sie ein *zusätzliches Bett/ Kinderbett* aufstellen?** ken'ən zē in *tsōō'zetslishəs bet/kin'dərbet* ouf'shtel'ən?
Do you have … room?	**Haben Sie noch ein … Zimmer?** hä'bən zē nôh in … tsim'ər?
another	**anderes** än'dərəs
a cheaper	**billigeres** bil'igərəs
a larger	**größeres** grē'sərəs
a quieter	**ruhigeres** rōō'igərəs
It's very nice. I'll take it.	**Es ist sehr schön. Ich nehme es.** es ist zār shēn. ish nā'mə es.

Can you have my luggage brought to the room?	**Können Sie mir das Gepäck aufs Zimmer bringen lassen?** ken'ən zē mēr däs gəpek' oufs tsim'ər bring'ən läs'ən?
Where can I park my car?	**Wo kann ich meinen Wagen parken?** vō kän ish mī'nən vä'gən pär'kən?
What are your mealtimes?	**Wann sind die Essenszeiten?** vän zint dē es'əns·tsī'tən?
Where is the dining room?	**Wo ist der Speisesaal?** vō ist där shpī'zəzäl'?
Can I have breakfast in my room?	**Kann ich auf dem Zimmer frühstücken?** kän ish ouf dām tsim'ər frē'shtikən?
Can I give you my valuables for safekeeping?	**Kann ich Ihnen meine Wertsachen zur Aufbewahrung geben?** kän ish ē'nən mī'nə värt'sähən tsōōr ouf'bəvä'rōōng gā'bən?
I'd like to pick up my valuables.	**Ich möchte meine Wertsachen abholen.** ish mesh'tə mīnə värt'sähən äp'hōlən.
Can you exchange money for me?	**Kann ich bei Ihnen Geld umtauschen?** kän ish bī ē'nən gelt ōōm'toushən?

| I'd like the key for room … | **Bitte den Schlüssel für Zimmer …** |
| | bit'ə dān shlüs'əl fēr tsim'ər … |

Could you please have this …	**Können Sie das bitte … lassen?**
	ken'ən zē däs bit'ə … läs'ən?
ironed?	**bügeln** bē'gəln
dry-cleaned?	**reinigen** rī'nigən
washed?	**waschen** väsh'ən

2

INFO Larger hotels usually provide a laundry service. If you wish something to be laundered, dry-cleaned or ironed, simply place the item of clothing in the plastic bag provided and cross off the service required on the blank. The chambermaid will take care of it and the charge will be added to your hotel check.

| Can I make a call to the U.S. (from my room)? | **Kann ich (von meinem Zimmer aus) nach Amerika telefonieren?** |
| | kän ish (fôn mī'nəm tsim'ər ous) näh ämā'rikä tālāfōnē'rən? |

| *Is there any mail/Are there any messages* for me? | **Ist *Post/eine Nachricht* für mich da?** |
| | ist *pôst/ī'nə näh'risht* fēr mish dä? |

| I'd like a wakeup call at … o'clock, please. | **Wecken Sie mich bitte um … Uhr.** |
| | vek'ən zē mish bit'ə ōōm … ōōr. |

We're leaving tomorrow.	**Wir reisen morgen ab.**
	vēr rī'zən môr'gən äp.
Would you please prepare my bill?	**Würden Sie bitte die Rechnung fertig machen?** vir'dən zē bit'ə dē resh'nŏŏng fer'tish mäh'ən?
May I leave my luggage here until ... o'clock?	**Kann ich mein Gepäck noch bis ... Uhr hier lassen?** kän ish mīn gəpek' nôh bis ... ŏŏr hēr läs'ən?
Would you call a taxi for me, please?	**Bitte rufen Sie mir ein Taxi.** bit'ə rŏŏ'fən zē mēr īn täk'sē.

INFO There are no hard and fast rules for tipping hotel staff. If you are staying for any length of time in one place we recommend you tip the chambermaid about 10 DM (70 Austrian shillings, 10 Swiss Francs) at some point. You will receive better attention if you do so. If you were very pleased with the standard of service in your hotel you can leave a tip for the whole staff at the desk.

Vacation Rental

| We have rented the apartment ... | **Wir haben die Wohnung ... gemietet.** |
| | vēr hä'bən dē vō'nŏŏng ... gəmē'tət |

Where can we pick up the keys?	**Wo bekommen wir die Schlüssel?** vō bəkôm'ən vēr dē shlis'əl?
Where is the *fusebox/meter*?	**Wo ist der *Sicherungskasten/ Stromzähler*?** vō ist dār zish'əroongs-kâs'tən/shtröm'tsālər?

INFO The electrical voltage is 220 volts. Plugs and sockets are also different from American ones. If you wish to use electrical appliances like shavers and hair dryers which you have brought with you you will need an adapter. These can be obtained either at the reception desk, from the chambermaid or at a store.

Could you please explain how the ... works?	**Könnten Sie uns bitte ... erklären?** ken'tən zē ōōns bit'ə ... erklā'rən?
dishwasher	**die Geschirrspülmaschine** dē gəshir'shpēlmäshē'nə
stove	**den Herd** dān hārd
washing machine	**die Waschmaschine** dē väsh'mäshe'nə
Where do we put the trash?	**Wohin kommt der Müll?** vōhin' kômt dār mil?

47

Where can I make a phone call?	**Wo kann man hier telefonieren?**
	vō kän män hēr tālāfōnē'rən?
Can you please tell us where ... is?	**Sagen Sie uns bitte, wo ... ist.**
	zä'gən zē ōōns bit'ə, vō ... ist.

the nearest bus stop
die nächste Bushaltestelle
dē nāsh'stə bōōs'hältəshtel'ə

the nearest subway station
die nächste U-Bahnstation
dē nāsh'stə ōō'bänstätsyōn`

a *grocery store/ supermarket*
ein *Lebensmittelgeschäft/ ein Supermarkt* īn lā'bənsmit'əl-gəsheft`/īn zōō'pərmärkt

Complaints

Could I please have ...?
Könnte ich bitte noch ... haben?
ken'tə ish bit'ə nōh ... hä'bən?

another blanket
eine Decke īnə dek'ə

some more dish towels
Geschirrtücher gəshir'tēshər

another hand towel
ein Handtuch īn hän'tōōh

a few more clothes hangers
ein paar Kleiderbügel īn pär klī'dərbē`gəl

another pillow
ein Kopfkissen īn kôpf'kisən

The window doesn't open/close.	**Das Fenster geht nicht *auf/zu*.** dặs fen'stər gāt nisht *ouf/tsōō.*
... doesn't work.	**... funktioniert nicht.** ... fōōngk'tsyōnērt' nisht.
The shower	**Die Dusche** dē dōō'shə
The TV	**Der Fernseher** dār fern'zā·ər
The heating	**Die Heizung** dē hī'tsōōng
The air conditioning	**Die Klimaanlage** dē klē'mä·än'lägə
The light	**Das Licht** dặs lisht
The fan	**Der Ventilator** dār ven'tēlä'tôr
The toilet doesn't flush.	**Die Wasserspülung funktioniert nicht.** dē vặs'ərshpē'lōōng fōōngk'tsyōnērt' nisht.
There is no (hot) water.	**Es kommt kein (warmes) Wasser.** es kômt kīn (vär'məs) vặs'ər.
The faucet drips.	**Der Wasserhahn tropft.** dār vặs'ərhän trôpft.
The drain/The toilet is stopped up.	***Der Abfluss/Die Toilette ist verstopft.*** dār ặp'flōōs/dē tô·ặlet'ə ist fershtôpft'.
... is dirty.	**... ist schmutzig.** ... ist shmōōts'ish.

2

INFO In Europe floor levels are labeled differently. If you wish to find the right level in your hotel you must know that the Europeans do not consider rooms at street level to be on the first floor. They start with „Erdgeschoss" (street level) and then number each floor accordingly. Thus the first floor (1. Stock) corresponds to the US second floor:

First floor   = Erdgeschoss (street level) ärt'gəshôs

Second floor = 1. Stock (first floor) er'stər shtôk

Third floor   = 2. Stock (second floor) tsvī'tər shtôk

etc.

Hotel and Vacation Rental

complaint	**die Beanstandung** dē bə·än'shtändoong
glass	**das Glas** däs gläs
hand towel	**das Handtuch** däs hän'tōōh
to have breakfast	**frühstücken** frē'shtikən
heating	**die Heizung** dē hī'tsoong
high season	**die Hauptsaison** dē houpt'säzôN'
hotel	**das Hotel** däs hōtel'
to iron clothes	**Wäsche bügeln** vesh'ə bē'gəln
key	**der Schlüssel** där shlis'əl
lamp	**die Lampe** dē läm'pə
laundry	**die Wäsche** dē vesh'ə
light	**das Licht** däs lisht

50

light bulb	**die Glühbirne** dē glē'bīrnə
light switch	**der Lichtschalter** där lisht'shältər
linens	**die Bettwäsche** dē bet'veshə
to look at	**ansehen** än'zā·ən
lounge	**der Aufenthaltsraum**
	där ouf'ent·hältsroum'
low season	**die Nachsaison** dē näh'sāzôN'
LP gas bottle	**die Gasflasche** dē gäs'fläshə
luggage	**das Gepäck** däs gəpek'
lunch	**das Mittagessen** däs mit'ägesən
maid	**das Zimmermädchen**
	däs tsim'əmäd'shən
mattress	**die Matratze** dē mäträts'ə
mirror	**der Spiegel** där shpē'gəl
nightstand	**der Nachttisch** där näht'ish
overnight stay	**die Übernachtung** dē ēbərnäh'tŏŏng
owner of the house	**der Hausbesitzer** där hous'bəzitsər
patio	**die Terrasse** dē teräs'ə
pillow	**das Kopfkissen** däs kôpf'kisən
plate	**der Teller** där tel'ər
pool	**der Swimmingpool** där svim'ingpōōl
pre-season	**die Vorsaison** dē fôr'sāzôN'
reception	**die Rezeption** dē rätseptsyōn'
reception area	**die Empfangshalle** dē empfängs'hälə
refrigerator	**der Kühlschrank** där kēl'shrängk
registration	**die Anmeldung** dē än'meldōōng

2

registration card	**der Anmeldeschein** dār än'meldəshīn`
rent	**die Miete** dē mē'tə
to rent	**mieten** mē'tən
to reserve	**reservieren** rāzervē'rən
room	**das Zimmer** däs tsim'ər
safe	**der Safe** dār zāf
sheet	**das Bettlaken** däs bet'läkən
shower	**die Dusche** dē dōōsh'ə
single bed	**das Einzelbett** däs īn'tsəlbet`
single room	**das Einzelzimmer** däs īn'tsəltsim`ər
sink	**das Waschbecken** däs väsh'bekən
steps	**die Treppe** dē trep'ə
stove	**der Herd** dār hārt
supper	**das Abendessen** däs ä'bənt·es`ən
table	**der Tisch** dār tish
(tele)phone	**das Telefon** däs tāləfōn'
toilet	**die Toilette** dē tô·älet'ə
toilet tissue	**das Toilettenpapier** däs tô·älet'ənpäpēr`
trash	**der Müll** dār mil
trash bin	**die Mülltonne** dē mil'tônə
trash can	**der Mülleimer** dār mil'īmər

INFO When disposing of trash please try to keep to the strict rules for doing so. Not only are there trash cans for domestic refuse but also various containers provided by local authorities for paper, plastic, organic matter, metal and different colors of glass bottles.

2

TV	**der Fernseher** dār fern'zā-ər
TV room	**der Fernsehraum** dār fern'zāroum
twin beds	**die zwei Einzelbetten** *(plural)*
	dē tsvī īn'tsəlbet'ən
vacation rental	**die Ferienwohnung**
	dē fā'rē-ənvō'nōōng
voltage	**die elektrische Spannung**
	dē ālek'trishə shpän'ōōng
to wake	**wecken** vek'ən
to wash clothes	**Wäsche waschen** vesh'ə väsh'ən
washing machine	**die Waschmaschine**
	dē väsh'mäshē'nə
waste basket	**der Papierkorb** dār päpēr'kôrp
water	**das Wasser** däs väs'ər
water faucet	**der Wasserhahn** dār väs'ərhän
window	**das Fenster** däs fens'tər
to work	**funktionieren** fōōngk'tsyōnē'rən

CAMPING

May we camp on your property?	**Dürfen wir auf Ihrem Grundstück zelten?** dir'fən vēr ouf ē'rəm grōōnt'shtĭk tsel'tən?
Do you still have room for …?	**Haben Sie noch Platz für …?** hä'bən zē nôh pläts fēr …?
What is the charge for …	**Wie hoch ist die Gebühr für …** vē hōh ist dē gəbēr' fēr …
… adults and … children?	**… Erwachsene und … Kinder?** … erväk'sənə ōōnt … kin'dər?
a car with camper?	**einen Pkw mit Wohnwagen?** i'nən pā'-kä-vä mit vōn'vägən?
a motorhome?	**ein Wohnmobil?** īn vōn'mōbēl?
a tent?	**ein Zelt?** īn tselt?
Do you also rent *cabins/campers*?	**Vermieten Sie auch *Bungalows/ Wohnwagen*?** fermē'tən zē ouh bōōng'gälōs/vōn'vägən?
We'd like a (protected) place in the shade.	**Wir möchten einen (windgeschützten) Platz im Schatten.** vēr mesh'tən i'nən (vint'gəshĭts'tən) pläts im shät'ən.

54

We'd like to stay one night/... nights.	**Wir möchten _einen Tag/... Tage_ bleiben**. vēr mẹsh'tən ī'nən täk/... tä'gə blī'bən.

Where can we _pitch our tent/set up our camper_?	**Wo können wir _unser Zelt/unseren Wohnwagen_ aufstellen?** vō kẹn'ən vēr ōōn'zər tselt/ōōn'zərən vōn'vägən ouf'shtelən?

Where are the _wash-rooms/rest rooms_?	**Wo sind die _Waschräume/Toiletten_?** vō zint dē väsh'roimə/tô·älet'ən?

Where can I ...	**Wo kann ich ...** vō kặn ịsh ...

flush out the camper waste water?	**das Chemieklo entsorgen?** däs shämē'klō entsôr'gən?
fill up with fresh water?	**Frischwasser nachfüllen?** frish'väsər näh'filən?
dump waste water?	**das Abwasser entsorgen?** däs ặp'väsər entsôr'gən?

Do you have power hookups here?	**Gibt es hier Stromanschluss?** gēpt es hēr shtrōm'ặnshlōōs?

Is there a grocery store here?	**Gibt es hier ein Lebensmittelgeschäft?** gēpt es hēr in lā'bənsmit'əlgəsheft'?

2

55

Can I *rent/exchange* LP gas tanks?	**Kann ich Gasflaschen *ausleihen/ umtauschen*?** kän i<u>sh</u> gäs'fläshən ous'lī·ən/ōōm'toushən?
May I borrow a(n) ..., please?	**Können Sie mir bitte ... leihen?** k<u>e</u>n'ən zē mēr bit'ə ...lī'ən?

INFO Germany alone has over 2000 campsites. We strongly recommend you book in advance at camp-sites during the peak season. Campsites are indicated by blue boards showing the international campsite sign of a black tent on a white background.

Camping guides are obtainable from all branches of the ADAC or from the Deutscher Camping Club (DCC) in Munich.

Camping

advance booking	**die Voranmeldung** dē fōr'änmel'dōōng
air mattress	**die Luftmatratze** dē lōōft'mäträts`ə
bed linens	**die Bettwäsche** dē bet'veshə
to borrow	**sich leihen** zi<u>sh</u> lī'ən
to camp	**zelten** tsel'tən
camper	**der Wohnwagen** dār vōn'vägən
camping	**das Camping** däs kem'ping
camping permit	**der Campingausweis** dār kem'pingous`vīs

campsite	**der Campingplatz** dār kem'pingpläts
check-in	**die Anmeldung** dē än'meldōōng
to check in	**sich anmelden** zish än'meldən
check-out	**die Abmeldung** dē äp'meldōōng
to check out	**sich abmelden** zish äp'meldən
chemical toilet	**das Chemieklo** däs shāmē'klō
clothes drier	**der Wäschetrockner** dār vesh'ətröknər
to cook	**kochen** kôh'ən
cooker	**der Kocher** dār kôh'ər
cooking utensils	**das Kochgeschirr** däs kôh'gəshir
crockery	**das Essgeschirr** däs es'gəshir
detergent	**das Waschmittel** däs väsh'mitəl
drinking water	**das Trinkwasser** däs tringk'väsər
electricity	**der Strom** dār shtröm
to empty	**entsorgen** entsôr'gən
fee	**die Benutzungsgebühr** dē bənōōts'ōōngsgəbēr'
to fill up with	**nachfüllen** näh'filən
foam (insulation) mat	**die Isomatte** dē ē'zōmät'ə
gas	**das Gas** däs gäs
gas bottle	**die Gasflasche** dē gäs'fläshə
gas canister	**die Gaskartusche** dē gäs'kärtōōsh'ə
gas cooker	**der Gaskocher** dār gäs'kôhər
gas lantern	**die Gaslampe** dē gäs'lämpə
membership card	**die Mitgliedskarte** dē mit'glēts·kär'tə

motor home	**das Wohnmobil** däs vōn'mōbēl
to park	**parken** pär'kən
playground	**der Spielplatz** dār shpēl'pläts
rental fee	**die Leihgebühr** dē lī'gəbēr
to rent out	**verleihen** fərlī'ən
saucepan	**der Kochtopf** dār kôḫ'tôpf
to set up	**aufstellen** ouf'shtelən
shower	**die Dusche** dē dōōsh'ə
to take a shower	**duschen** dōōsh'ən
sleeping bag	**der Schlafsack** dār shläf'säk
tent	**das Zelt** däs tselt
tent peg	**der Hering** dār hā'ring
tent pole	**die Zeltstange** dē tselt'shtängə
toilet	**die Toilette** dē tô-älet'ə
washing machine	**die Waschmaschine** dē väsh'mäshē nə
washroom	**der Waschraum** dār väsh'roum
to wash	**waschen** väsh'ən
water	**das Wasser** däs väs'ər
water canister	**der Wasserkanister** dār väs'ərkänis'tər

On the Way

ASKING THE WAY

Excuse me, where is ...?	**Entschuldigung, wo ist ...?**	entschool'digoong, vō ist ...?
What's the *quickest/cheapest* way to get to the ...	**Wie komme ich am *schnellsten/billigsten* zum ...**	vē kôm'ə ish äm shnel'stən/bil'igstən tsōōm ...
train station?	**Bahnhof?**	bän'hōf?
bus terminal?	**Busbahnhof?**	bōōs'bänhōf?
airport?	**Flughafen?**	flōōk'häfən?
How do I get to the highway?	**Wie komme ich zur Autobahn?**	vē kôm'ə ish tsōōr ou'tōbän?

❗ •	**Tut mir Leid, das weiß ich nicht.** tōōt mēr līt, däs vīs ish nisht.	I'm afraid I don't know.
❗ •	**Geradeaus.** gərä'də·ous'.	Straight ahead.
❗ •	**Nach rechts.** näh reshts.	To the right.
❗ •	**Nach links.** näh lingks.	To the left.
❗ •	**Die *erste/zweite* Straße *links/rechts*.** dē ers'tə/tsvī'tə shträ'sə lingks/reshts.	The *first/second* street to the *left/right*.
❗ •	**Nach der Kreuzung.** näh dār kroi'tsōōng.	After the intersection.

! **Überqueren Sie ...** ēbərkvā'rən   Cross ...

• zē ...

    die Brücke! dē brīk'ə.   the bridge.
    die Straße! dē shträ'sə.   the street.

! **Dann fragen Sie noch einmal.**   Then ask again.

• dän frä'gən zē nôḫ īn'mäl.

! **Sie können** *den Bus/die U-Bahn*   You can take the

• **nehmen.** zē ken'ən *dān* bōōs/dē   *bus/subway.*
    ōō'bän nā'mən.

Is this the road to ...?   **Ist dies die Straße nach ...?**
       ist dēs dē shträ'sə näḫ ...?

How far is it?   **Wie weit ist es?** vē vīt ist es?

! **Nicht weit.** niḫt vīt.   Not (very) far.

How many minutes *on*   **Wie viele Minuten** *zu Fuß/mit dem*
foot/by car?   *Auto?* vē fē'lə minōō'tən tsōō fōōs/mit
       dām ou'tō?

! **Ganz in der Nähe.** gänts in dār   It's very nearby.
    nā'ə.

Could you show me   **Zeigen Sie mir das bitte auf der**
on the map?   **Karte.** tsī'gən zē mēr däs bit'ə ouf dār
       kär'tə.

3

61

AT THE BORDER

Passport Control

❗ Ihren Pass, bitte. ē'rən päs, bit'ə. Your passport, please.

❓ Wie lange bleiben Sie hier? How long will you be
vē läng'ə blī'bən zē hēr? staying?

❓ Was ist der Zweck Ihrer Reise? What is the purpose
väs ist dār tsvek ē'rər rī'zə? of your visit?

I'm with the ... group. **Ich gehöre zur Reisegruppe ...**
ish gəhā'rə tsōōr rī'zəgrōōpə ...

Customs

❓ Haben Sie etwas zu verzollen? Do you have anything
hä'bən zē et'väs tsōō fərtsôl'ən? to declare?

I only have *personal* **Ich habe nur *Sachen für meinen***
items/presents. ***persönlichen Bedarf/Geschenke.***
ish hä'bə nōōr *zäh'ən fēr mī'nən*
pərzān'lishən bədärf/gəsheng'kə.

❗ Öffnen Sie bitte den Koffer. Open the suitcase,
ef'nən zē bit'ə dān kôf'ər. please.

❗ Das müssen Sie verzollen. You'll have to pay
däs müs'ən zē fərtsôl'ən. duty on that.

62

INFO The EU (European Union), which, by the way, Switzerland doesn't belong to, has no border controls as restrictions within member countries have been relaxed for some time now. However, it is still necessary to carry a valid passport or ID around with you. Passport controls are still carried out, perhaps even more strictly than before, at borders to non-EU member countries.

At the border

bill	**die Rechnung**	dē resh'nōōng
border	**die Grenze**	dē gren'tsə
certificate	**das Zertifikat**	däs tsertifikät'
customs	**der Zoll**	dār tsôl
customs agent	**der Zollbeamte**	dār tsôl'be·äm`tə
customs declaration	**die Zollerklärung**	dē tsôl'erklä`rōōng
customs office	**das Zollamt**	däs tsôl'ämt
documents	**die Papiere** *(plural)*	dē päpē'rə
expired	**abgelaufen**	äp'gəlou`fən
first name	**der Vorname**	dār fōr'nämə
inoculation record	**der Impfpass**	dār impf'päs
invalid	**ungültig**	ōōn'giltish
journey	**die Reise**	dē rī'zə
nationality	**die Staatsangehörigkeit**	
	dē shtäts'ängəhā`rishkīt	
papers	**die Papiere** *(plural)*	dē päpē'rə

to pay duty on	**verzollen** fərtsôl'ən
place of residence	**der Wohnort** dār vōn'ôrt
to renew	**verlängern** fərleng'ərn
signature	**die Unterschrift** dē ŏŏn'tərshrift
surname	**der Familienname** dār fámē'lē-ənä'mə
travel group	**die Reisegruppe** dē rī'zəgrŏŏpə
trip	**die Reise** dē rī'zə
valid	**gültig** gil'tish
visa	**das Visum** däs vē'zŏŏm

PLANE

Information and Booking

Which terminal do I need if I'm flying with ... to ...?	**Zu welchem Terminal muss ich, wenn ich mit ... nach ... fliegen möchte?** tsŏŏ vel'shəm tĕr'minəl mŏŏs ish, ven ish mit ... näh ... flē'gən mesh'tə?
Where is the ... counter?	**Wo ist der ... Schalter?** vō ist dār ... shäl'tər?
When is the next flight to ...?	**Wann fliegt die nächste Maschine nach ...?** vän flēkt dē näsh'stə mäshē'nə näh ...?

How much is the (round-trip) fare to ...?	**Wie viel kostet ein Flug nach ... (und zurück)?** vē fēl kôs'tət in flōōk näh ... (ōōnt tsōōrik')?
I'd like a ticket to ..., ...	**Bitte ein Flugticket nach ..., ...** bit'ə in flōōk'tikət näh ..., ...

one way.	**einfach.** īn'fäh.
round-trip.	**hin und zurück.** hin ōōnt tsōōrik'.
economy class.	**Economy class.** ikôn'əmē kläs.
first-class.	**1. Klasse.** ers'tər kläs'ə.

! **Dieser Flug ist leider ausgebucht.** I'm afraid this flight
dē'zər flōōk ist lī'dər ous'gəbōōht.   is booked out.

Are there any *special rates/stand-by seats* available?	**Gibt es *Sondertarife/Stand-by-Plätze*?** gēpt es zôn'dərtärē'fə/stend-bī'- plet'sə?

3

INFO Scheduled domestic flights in Germany are very
expensive. However, cut-rate fares for domestic
flights between major cities are available. The price of these
flights can work out cheaper than special-rate rail fares. We
advise you to make enquiries about special discounts at travel
agencies.

I'd like *a window seat/* **Ich hätte gerne einen *Fensterplatz/***
an aisle seat. ***Platz am Gang.*** i<u>sh</u> het'ə ger'nə ī'nən
fens'tərpläts/pläts äm gäng.

> **!** **Dies ist ein Nichtraucherflug.** This is a non-smoking
> **●** dēs ist īn ni<u>sh</u>t'rou<u>h</u>ərflook'. flight.

INFO In general, in Germany people are more tolerant of
smokers than in the USA. However, in restaurants
and airports etc. you will come across smoke-free zones more and
more frequently. Smoking is mostly prohibitted on public transport within towns and on Lufthansa domestic flights.
The German railroad company (Bundesbahn) provides both
smoking and non-smoking cars.

Can I take this as **Kann ich das als Handgepäck**
carry-on baggage? **mitnehmen?** kän i<u>sh</u> däs äls
hänt'gəpek mit'nāmən?

I'd like to ... my flight. **Ich möchte diesen Flug ...** i<u>sh</u>
mē<u>sh</u>'tə dē'zən flook ...

confirm **bestätigen lassen.** bəshtä'tigən
läs'ən.

cancel **stornieren.** shtôrnē'rən.

change **umbuchen.** oom'boohən.

Where is Gate B?	**Wo ist der Ausgang B?** vō ist dār ous'gäng bā?
My baggage has been damaged.	**Mein Koffer ist beschädigt worden.** mīn kôf'ər ist bəshā'dikt vôr'dən.

On the Plane

Could I have (*another/ some more*) …, please?	**Könnte ich bitte (*noch ein/noch etwas*) … bekommen?** ken'tə ish bit'ə (nôh īn/nôh et'väs) … bəkôm'ən?
I feel sick.	**Mir ist schlecht.** mēr ist shlesht.

Plane

3

airline	**die Fluggesellschaft** dē flōōk'gəzel'shäft
airplane	**das Flugzeug** däs flōōk'tsoik
airport	**der Flughafen** dār flōōk'häfən
airport shuttle bus	**der Flughafenbus** dār flōōk'häfənbōōs'
airsickness	**die Luftkrankheit** dē lōōft'krängk'hīt
arrival	**die Ankunft** dē än'kōōnft
baggage	**das Gepäck** däs gəpek'
boarding pass	**die Bordkarte** dē bôrt'kärtə
to book	**buchen** bōō'hən
booking	**die Buchung** dē bōō'hōōng
carry-on baggage	**das Handgepäck** däs hänt'gəpek'

counter	**der Schalter** där shäl'tər
child-care room	**der Wickelraum** där vik'əlroum
class	**die Klasse** dē kläs'ə
to confirm	**bestätigen** bəshtä'tigən
connecting flight	**der Anschlussflug** där än'shlōōsflōōk´
delay	**die Verspätung** de fərshpä'tōōng
departure	**der Abflug** där äp'flōōk
emergency chute	**die Notrutsche** dē nōt'rōōtshə
emergency exit	**der Notausgang** där nōt'ousgäng
emergency landing	**die Notlandung** dē nōt'ländōōng
exit	**der Ausgang** där ous'gäng
to fasten one's seatbelt	**sich anschnallen** zish än'shnälən
flight	**der Flug** där flōōk
flight attendant	**der Steward; die Stewardess** där styōō'ərt; dē styōō'ərdes
to fly	**fliegen** flē'gən
flying time	**die Flugzeit** dē flōōk'tsīt
fresh air inlet	**die Frischluftdüse** dē frish'lōōftdē´zə
hand baggage	**das Handgepäck** däs hänt'gəpek
information desk	**der Informationsschalter** där infôr-mätsyōns'shältər
to land	**landen** län'dən
landing	**die Landung** dē län'dōōng
life jacket	**die Schwimmweste** dē shvim'vestə
local time	**die Ortszeit** dē ôrts'tsīt

nonsmoking section	**der Nichtraucher** dār nisht'rouhər
reservation	**die Buchung** dē bōō'hōong
to make a reservation	**buchen** bōō'hən
return flight	**der Rückflug** dār rik'flook
scheduled flight	**der Linienflug** dār lē'nē·ənflook'
sick bag	**die Spucktüte** dē shpook'tētə
smoking section	**der Raucher** dār rou'hər
stopover	**die Zwischenlandung** dē tsvish'ənlándoong
take-off	**der Start** dār shtärt
to take off	**starten** shtär'tən
vegetarian meal	**das vegetarische Essen** däs vegetä'rishə es'ən

RAIL

Information and Tickets

Where can I find the *checkroom/lockers*?

Wo finde ich die *Gepäckaufbe-wahrung/Schließfächer?* vō fin'də ish dē gapek'oufbavä'rōong/shlēs'feshər?

When is the *next/last* train to …?	**Wann fährt der *nächste/letzte* Zug nach …?** vän färt dār *nāsh'stə/lets'tə* tsōōk näh …?
Do I have to change trains?	**Muss ich umsteigen?** mōōs ish ōōm'shtigən?
Which platform does the train to … leave from?	**Von welchem Gleis fährt der Zug nach … ab?** fôn vel'shəm glīs färt dār tsōōk näh … äp?
What is the fare to …?	**Was kostet die Fahrt nach …?** väs kôs'tət dē färt näh …?
Are there special rates for …?	**Gibt es eine Ermäßigung für …?** gēpt es ī'nə ermä'sigōōng fēr …?
I'd like a.. ticket to Berlin, please.	**Bitte eine Fahrkarte nach Berlin, …** bit'ə ī'nə fär'kärtə näh berlēn', …
one way	**einfach.** īn'fäh.
round-trip	**hin und zurück.** hin ōōnt tsōōrik'.
first/second class	***erster/zweiter* Klasse.** ers'tər/ tsvī'tər kläs'ə.
I'd like to reserve a seat … on the 8 o'clock train to Berlin, please.	**Bitte reservieren Sie für den Zug nach Berlin um 8 Uhr einen Platz …** bit'ə rāzervē'rən zē fēr dān tsōōk näh berlēn' ōōm … ōōr ī'nən pläts …

70

by the window	**am Fenster.** ăm fens'tər.
in nonsmoking	**im Nichtraucherabteil.** im
	nisht'rouhərăptîl'.
in smoking	**im Raucherabteil.** fĕr rou'hərăptîl'.

INFO There is an excellent railroad network between large cities at hourly intervals. The fastest trains are the ICE (Intercity Express), the IC (Intercity) and the EC (Eurocity); there is a surcharge on these trains. The IR (Interregio/Interregional Train) makes frequent stops and is therefore slower. The slowest trains are the RE trains (Regional Trains) which stop at every little village. Buses are used to reach the far-out places where it isn't economical to run a train service. The tickets (and any surcharges) are paid for in advance at station ticket desks or in travel agencies. There is a wide range of special rates, some with conditions attached. One of these rates is for runaround tickets either lasting a few days or a month. With these tickets you can enjoy unlimited travel within Germany.

3

Signs

Ausgang ous'găng	Exit
Auskunft ous'kŏŏnft	Information
Bahnhofsgaststätte	Restaurant
bän'hōfsgäst'shtetə	
Bahnsteig bän'shtīk	Platform

Fundbüro foont'bĕrō	Lost-and-Found
Gepäckannahme gəpek'änä'mə	Baggage Check-In
Gepäckaufbewahrung gəpek'- oufbəvä'rōong	Checkroom
Gleis glīs	Track
Schließfächer shlēs'feshər	Lockers
Toiletten tô-älet'ən	Rest Rooms
Wartesaal vär'təzäl	Waiting Room
Zu den Bahnsteigen tsōō dān bän'shtīgən	To All Trains

On the Train

Is this seat taken?	**Ist dieser Platz frei?** ist dē'zər pläts frī?
Excuse me, but I believe this is my seat.	**Entschuldigen Sie, ich glaube, dies ist mein Platz.** entshōōl'digən zē, ish glou'bə, dēs ist mīn pläts.
Could you help me, please?	**Können Sie mir bitte helfen?** ken'ən zē mēr bit'ə hel'fən?
! **Die Fahrkarten, bitte!** dē fär'kärtən, bit'ə!	Tickets, please!
How many more stops to …?	**Wie viele Stationen sind es noch bis …?** vē fē'lə shtätsyō'nən zint es nôḫ bis …?

How long is our layover?	**Wie lange haben wir Aufenthalt?** vē läng'ə hä'bən vēr ouf'ent·hält'?

Train

arrival	**die Ankunft** dē än'kŏŏnft
to arrive	**ankommen** än'kómən
baggage car	**der Gepäckwagen** dār gəpek'vägən
to board	**einsteigen** īn'shtīgən
car	**der Waggon** dār vägôN'
class	**die Klasse** dē kläs'ə
to change (trains)	**umsteigen** ŏŏm'shtīgən
compartment	**das Abteil** däs äptīl'
conductor	**der Schaffner** dār shäf'nər
connection	**der Anschluss** dār än'shlŏŏs
to depart	**abfahren** äp'färən
departure	**die Abfahrt** dē äp'färt
dining car	**der Speisewagen** dār shpī'zəvägən
emergency brake	**die Notbremse** dē nōt'bremzə
to get off	**aussteigen** ous'shtīgən
to get on	**einsteigen** īn'shtīgən
to go (by train)	**(mit dem Zug) fahren** (mit dām tsōōk) fä'rən
to leave	**abfahren** äp'färən
lockers	**die Schließfächer** *(plural)* dē shlēs'feshər

nonsmoker	**der Nichtraucher** dār ni<u>sh</u>t'rou<u></u>hər
occupied	**besetzt** bəzetst'
open seating car	**der Großraumwagen** dār grōs'roum- vä'gən
platform	**der Bahnsteig** dār bän'shtīk
reserved	**reserviert** räzervērt'
seat	**der Platz** dār plä<u></u>ts
sleeping car	**der Liegewagen, der Schlafwagen** dār lē'gəvägən, dār shläf'vägən
smoker	**der Raucher** dār rou'hər
special rate	**die Ermäßigung** dē ermä'sigōong
taken	**besetzt** bəzetst'
ticket	**die Fahrkarte** dē fär'kärtə
timetable	**der Fahrplan** dār fär'plän
track	**das Gleis** dä<u></u>s glīs
train	**der Zug** dār tsōōk
train station	**der Bahnhof** dār bän'hōf

LONG-DISTANCE BUSES

| Is there a bus service
to …? | **Gibt es eine Busverbindung nach …?**
gēpt es ī'nə bōōs'fərbin`dōōng nä<u>h</u> …? |
| Where do I have to
change? | **Wo muss ich umsteigen?** vō mōōs
i<u>sh</u> ōōm'shtīgən? |

Would you please tell me when we'll get to …?	**Würden Sie mir bitte sagen, wann wir in … sind?** vir'dən zē mēr bit'ə zä'gən, vän vēr in … zint?
Is there a rest room on this bus?	**Gibt es eine Toilette in diesem Bus?** gēpt es ī'nə tō·älet'ə in dē'zəm bōōs?
How long is our layover here?	**Wie lange haben wir hier Aufenthalt?** vē läng'ə hä'bən vēr hēr ouf'enthält`?
Is this seat taken?	**Ist dieser Platz frei?** ist dē'zər pläts frī?
Do you mind if I sit next to you?	**Darf ich mich zu Ihnen setzen?** därf ish mish tsōō ē'nən zets'ən?

3

CAR, MOTORBIKE AND BIKE

Rentals

I'd like to rent a … (with automatic).	**Ich möchte … (mit Automatik) mieten.** ish mesh'tə … (mit outōmä'tik) mē'tən.
car	**ein Auto** īn ou'tō
sport utility	**einen Geländewagen** ī'nən gəlen'dəvägən
minivan	**einen Kleinbus** ī'nən klīn'bōōs
RV	**ein Wohnmobil** īn vōn'mōbēl

75

| How many kilometers are included in the price? | **Wie viele Kilometer sind im Preis inbegriffen?** vē fē'lə kilōmā'tər zint im prīs inbəgrif'ən? |

! Kann ich bitte Ihren (internationalen) Führerschein sehen? kän ish bit'ə ē'rən (intərnäts'- yōnä'lən) fē'rərshīn zā'ən?

Can I see your (inter- national) driver's license, please?

| I'd like to rent a bicycle/mountain bike. | **Ich möchte ein _Fahrrad/Mountain- bike_ mieten.** ish mesh'tə īn _fä'rät/ moun'tənbīk_ mē'tən. |

| I'd like to rent it for … | **Ich möchte es für … mieten.** ish mesh'tə es fēr … mē'tən. |

tomorrow.	**morgen** môr'gən
the day after tomorrow.	**übermorgen** ē'bərmôrgən
one day.	**einen Tag** ī'nən täk
two days.	**zwei Tage** tsvī tä'gə
one week.	**eine Woche** ī'nə vôh'ə

! Was für einen Wagen möchten Sie? väs fēr ī'nən vä'gən mesh'tən zē?

What kind of car would you like?

| What kind of fuel does it take? | **Was muss ich tanken?** väs mōōs ish täng'kən? |

76

Is comprehensive insurance included?	**Ist eine Vollkaskoversicherung eingeschlossen?** ist ī'nə fôl'käskō-fərzish`ərŏŏng in'gəshlôsən?
What's the deductible	**Wie hoch ist die Selbstbeteiligung?** vē hōh ist dē zelpst'bətī`ligŏŏng?
Can I turn in the car in …?	**Kann ich das Auto auch in … abgeben?** kän ish däs ou'tō ouh in … äp'gäbən?
I'd also like a helmet.	**Bitte geben Sie mir auch einen Sturzhelm.** bit'ə gä'bən zē mēr ouh ī'nən shtŏŏrts'helm.

3

INFO In built-up areas you must honor the 50 km/h speed limit. On country routes or secondary roads the speed limit is 100 km/h. On the German autobahn (highway) there is no general speed limit, although it is advised not to exceed a top speed of 110 km/h.

The speed limit on the Austrian autobahn (toll highway) is 130 km/h.

On the Swiss autobahn (toll highway) it is 120 km/h.

| General guide: | **1 kilometer = 0.6214 miles** |
| As a rough guide: | **50 miles = 80 kilometers** |

Parking

Is there a *parking garage/parking lot* nearby?	**Ist hier in der Nähe ein *Parkhaus/Parkplatz*?** ist hēr in dār nā'ə in pärk'hous/pärk'pläts?
Is the parking garage open all night?	**Ist das Parkhaus die ganze Nacht geöffnet?** ist däs pärk'hous dē gän'tsə nä̲ht gə·ef'nət?
Can I park here?	**Kann ich hier parken?** kän i̲sh hēr pär'kən?

Gas Stations, Car Repair

Where is/How far is it to the nearest gas station?	**Wo/Wie weit ist die nächste Tankstelle?** vō/vē vīt ist dē nä̲sh'stə tängk'shtelə?
Fill it up, please.	**Bitte voll tanken!** bit'ə fôl täng'kən.
... dollars' worth of *unleaded/Super unleaded*, please.	**Bitte für ... Mark *Benzin/Super* bleifrei.** bit'ə fēr ... märk bentsēn'/zōō'pər blī'frī.
I'd like *1 quart/2 quarts* of oil, please.	**Ich möchte *1 Liter/2 Liter* Öl.** i̲sh me̲sh'tə i'nən lē'tər/tsvī lē'tər ȫl.
I need snow chains.	**Ich brauche Schneeketten.** i̲sh brou'hə shnā'ketən.

78

Breakdown and Accidents

Please call …, quickly!	**Rufen Sie bitte schnell …** rōō'fən zē bit'ə shnel …
the fire department	**die Feuerwehr!** dē foi'ərvār.
an ambulance	**einen Krankenwagen!** ī'nən kräng'kənvägən.
the police	**die Polizei!** dē pōlitsī'.
I've had an accident.	**Ich habe einen Unfall gehabt.** ish hä'bə ī'nən ōōn'fäl gəhäpt.
May I use your phone?	**Kann ich bei Ihnen telefonieren?** kän ish bī ē'nən tālāfōnē'rən?
Nobody's hurt.	**Es ist niemand verletzt.** es ist nē'mänt fərletst'.
… people have been (seriously) hurt.	**… Personen sind (schwer) verletzt.** … perzō'nən zint (shvār) fərletst'.
Please help me.	**Bitte helfen Sie mir.** bit'ə hel'fən zē mēr.
I need some bandages.	**Ich brauche Verbandszeug.** ish brou'hə fərbän'tsoik.
I'm out of gas.	**Ich habe kein Benzin mehr.** ish hä'bə kīn bentsēn' mār.

3

Could you …	**Könnten Sie …** kẹn'tən zē …
give me a lift?	**mich ein Stück mitnehmen?** mi<u>sh</u> īn shtĭk mĭt'nāmən?
tow my car?	**meinen Wagen abschleppen?** mī'nən vä'gən äp'shlepən?
send me a wrecker?	**mir einen Abschleppwagen schicken?** mēr ī'nən äp'shlepvä'gən shĭk'ən?

I was doing … kilometers per hour.	**Ich bin … Kilometer in der Stunde gefahren.** i<u>sh</u> bĭn … kĭlōmā'tər ĭn dār shtōōn'də gəfä'rən.

May I have *your name and address/your insurance information*, please.	**Bitte geben sie mir *Ihren Namen und Ihre Adresse/Ihre Versicherung* an.** bĭt'ə gā'bən zē mēr ē'rən nä'mən ōōnt ē'rə ädres'ə/ē'rə fərzĭ<u>sh</u>'ərōōng än.

Here is *my name and address/my insurance information*.	**Hier ist *mein Name und meine Adresse/meine Versicherung*.** hēr ĭst mīn nä'mə ōōnt mī'nə ädres'ə/mī'nə fərzĭ<u>sh</u>'ərōōng.

| Thank you very much for your help. | **Vielen Dank für Ihre Hilfe.** fē'lən dängk f
ür ē're hĭl'fə. |
|---|---|

Ihre Papiere bitte.
ē're päpē'rə bit'ə.

Your driver's license, registration, and insurance information, please.

INFO The AAA equivalent in Germany is the ADAC, in Austria the ÖAMTC and the ACS in Switzerland. If you have a breakdown these automobile associations will help you at all times, even if you are not a member. On the German autobahn there are emergency phones at regular intervals for you to contact the police or a breakdown service free of charge.

Do it yourself

3

Could you lend me ..., please?	**Können Sie mir bitte ... leihen?** ken'ən zē mēr bit'ə ... lī'ən?
some string	**Bindfaden** bint'fädən
a bicycle repair kit	**Fahrradflickzeug** fä'rätflik'tsoik
a cable	**ein Kabel** īn kä'bəl
a pump	**eine Luftpumpe** ī'nə lōōft'pōōmpə
some sandpaper	**Schmirgelpapier** shmir'gəlpäpēr'
a (...) screw	**eine Schraube (Größe ...)** ī'nə shrou'bə (grᾱ'sə ...)
a (...) wrench	**einen Schraubenschlüssel (Größe ...)** ī'nən shrou'bənshlisəl (grᾱ'sə ...)

81

a screwdriver	**einen Schraubenzieher** ī'nən shrou'bəntsē·ər
a funnel	**einen Trichter** ī'nən tri<u>sh</u>'tər
a jack	**einen Wagenheber** ī'nən vä'gənhäbər
a tool kit	**Werkzeug** värk'tsoik
a pair of pliers	**eine Zange** ī'nə tsäng'ə

At the Repair Shop

Where is the nearest (Ford *etc.*) garage?	**Wo ist die nächste (Ford *etc.*) Werk-statt?** vō ist dē nä<u>sh</u>'stə (fôrt *etc.*) värk'shtät?
My car's on the road to …	**Mein Wagen steht an der Straße nach …** mīn vä'gən shtāt än dār shträ'sə nä<u>h</u> …
Can you tow it away?	**Können Sie ihn abschleppen?** kœn'ən zē ēn äp'shlepən?
… is broken/doesn't work.	**… ist kaputt/geht nicht mehr.** … ist käpoōt'/gāt ni<u>sh</u>t mār.
My car won't start.	**Mein Auto springt nicht an.** mīn ou'tō shpringt ni<u>sh</u>t än.
The battery is dead.	**Die Batterie ist leer.** dē bätərē' ist lār.

The engine *sounds funny/doesn't have any power.*	**Der Motor *klingt merkwürdig/zieht nicht.*** dār mōtōr' klingt mārk'vịrdish/ tsēt nisht.
Just do the essential repairs, please.	**Machen Sie bitte nur die nötigsten Reparaturen.** mäh'ən zē bit'ə nōōr də nä'tish·stən repärätōō'rən.
Can I still drive it?	**Kann ich damit noch fahren?** kän ish dä'mit nōh fä'rən?
When will it be ready?	**Wann ist es fertig?** vän ist er fer'tish?

Car, Motorbike and Bike

3

accelerator	**das Gaspedal** däs gäs'pedäl'
accident	**der Unfall** dār ōōn'fäl
accident report	**das Unfallprotokoll** däs ōōn'fälprōtō-kōl'
antifreeze	**das Frostschutzmittel** däs frôst'shōōtsmit'əl
automatic (transmission)	**die Automatik** də outōmä'tik
battery	**die Batterie** də bätərē'
bicycle	**das Fahrrad** däs fä'rät
body damage	**der Blechschaden** dār blesh'shädən
brake	**die Bremse** də brem'zə
brake light	**das Bremslicht** däs brems'lisht

brake pedal	**das Bremspedal** däs brems'pedäl'
brights	**das Fernlicht** däs fern'lisht
broken	**kaputt** käpŏŏt'
bulb	**die Glühbirne** dē glē'birnə
bumper	**die Stoßstange** dē shtös'shtängə
car	**das Auto** däs ou'tō
car key	**der Autoschlüssel** där ou'tōshljsəl
casualty	**der Verletzte** där ferlets'tə
catalytic converter	**der Katalysator** där kät'äljzä'tôr
children's seat	**der Kindersitz** där kin'dərzits
clutch	**die Kupplung** dē kŏŏp'lŏŏng
collision	**der Zusammenstoß** där tsŏŏzäm'ənshtōs
coolant	**das Kühlwasser** däs kēl'väsər
country road	**die Landstraße** dē länt'shträsə
crash	**der Zusammenstoß** där tsŏŏzäm'ənshtōs
curve	**die Kurve** dē kŏŏr'və
distilled water	**das destillierte Wasser** däs destilēr'tə väs'ər
documents	**die Papiere** *(plural)* dē päpē'rə
to drive	**fahren** fä'rən
driver's license	**der Führerschein** där fē'rərshīn
emergency brake	**die Handbremse** dē hänt'bremzə
emergency triangle	**das Warndreieck** däs värn'drī'ek
engine	**der Motor** där mōtôr'

exhaust	**der Auspuff**	där ous'poof
expressway	**die Schnellstraße**	dē shnel'shträsə
fanbelt	**der Keilriemen**	där kīl'rēmən
fender	**der Kotflügel**	där köt'flēgəl
fire extinguisher	**der Feuerlöscher**	där foi'ərleshər
first-aid kit	**der Verbandskasten**	där fərbänts'-kästən
flasher	**das Blinklicht**	däs blingk'lisht
flat tire	**die Reifenpanne**	dē rī'fənpänə
four-wheel drive	**der Geländewagen**	där gəlen'dəvägən
fuse	**die Sicherung**	dē zish'əroong
garage	**die Werkstatt**	dē värk'shtät
gas	**das Benzin**	däs bentsēn'
gas pedal	**das Gaspedal**	däs gäs'pedäl'
gas station	**die Tankstelle**	dē tängk'shtelə
gear	**der Gang**	där gäng
gearshift lever	**der Schaltknüppel**	där shält'knipəl
to get gas	**tanken**	täng'kən
handbrake	**die Handbremse**	dē hänt'bremzə
to have a look at	**nachsehen**	näh'zā-ən
headlights	**die Scheinwerfer** *(plural)*	dē shīn'värfər
heating	**die Heizung**	dē hī'tsooong
highway	**die Autobahn**	dē ou'tōbän
hood	**die Motorhaube**	dē mō'tōrhou`bə
horn	**die Hupe**	dē hoo'pə

3

hubcap	**die Radkappe** dē rät'käpə	
idling	**im Leerlauf** im lār'louf	
injured	**verletzt** fərletst'	
injured person	**der Verletzte** dār fərlets'tə	
injury	**die Verletzung** dē fərlet'sōōng	
insurance	**die Versicherung** dē fərzi<u>sh</u>'ərōōng	
intersection	**das Autobahnkreuz** däs ou'tō-bän·kroits'	
jumper cables	**das Starthilfekabel** däs shtärt'hilfəkä'bəl	
lead-free	**bleifrei** blī'frī	
to let off the gas	**Gas wegnehmen** gäs vek'nāmən	
license number	**die Autonummer** dē ou'tōnōōmər	
low-beams	**das Abblendlicht** däs äp'blentli<u>sh</u>t	
minivan	**der Kleinbus** dār klīn'bōōs	
motor	**der Motor** dār mōtōr'	
motor home	**das Wohnmobil** däs vōn'mōbēl'	
motorcycle	**das Motorrad** däs mōtōr'ät	
no parking	**das Parkverbot** däs pärk'fərbōt	
off-ramp	**die Autobahnausfahrt** dē ou'tōbän·ous'färt	
oil	**das Motoröl** däs mō'tōrāl	
on-ramp	**die Autobahnauffahrt** dē ou'tōbän·ou'färt	
outside mirror	**der Außenspiegel** dār ou'sənshpēgəl	
paint	**der Lack** dār läk	

to park	**parken** pär'kən
parking garage	**das Parkhaus** däs pärk'hous
parking light	**das Standlicht** däs shtänt'li<u>sh</u>t
parking lot	**der Parkplatz** dār pärk'pläts
parking meter	**die Parkuhr** dē pärk'o͞or
pressure	**der Reifendruck** dār rī'fəndro͞ok
radiator	**der Kühler** dār kē'lər
rear-end collision	**der Auffahrunfall** dār ou'fär-o͞on'fäl
rear-view mirror	**der Rückspiegel** dār rik'shpēgəl
to rent	**mieten** mē'tən
to repair	**reparieren** repärē'rən
reverse (gear)	**der Rückwärtsgang** dār rik'vertsgäng
right of way	**die Vorfahrt** dē fôr'färt
road atlas	**der Autoatlas** dār ou'tō-ät'läs
RV	**das Wohnmobil** däs vōn'mōbēl'
seatbelt	**der Sicherheitsgurt** dār zi<u>sh</u>'ərhītsgo͞ort'
secondary road	**die Landstraße** dē länt'shträsə
service area	**die Raststätte** dē räst'shtetə
shoulder	**die Standspur** dē shtänt'shpo͞or
to sound the horn	**hupen** ho͞o'pən
spare part	**das Ersatzteil** däs erzäts'tīl
spare tire	**der Reservereifen** dār rezär'vərifən
speedometer	**der Tacho(meter)** dār tä<u>h</u>'ō(mä'tər)
sport utility vehicle	**der Geländewagen** dār gəlen'dəvägən
starter	**der Anlasser** dār än'läsər
steering	**die Lenkung** dē leng'ko͞ong

3

to step on the gas	**Gas geben** gäs gā'bən
sunroof	**das Schiebedach** däs shē'bədäh
switch	**der Schalter** dār shäl'tər
tail light	**das Schlusslicht** däs shlōōs'lisht
tire	**der Reifen** dēr rī'fən
toll	**die Maut** dē mout
toll booth	**die Mautstelle** dē mout'shtelə
toll road	**die mautpflichtige Straße** dē
	mout'pflish`tigə shträ'sə
to tow (off)	**abschleppen** äp'shlepən
tow rope	**das Abschleppseil** däs äp'shlepsīl`
transmission	**das Getriebe** däs gətrē'bə
turn indicator	**das Blinklicht** däs blingk'lisht
to turn in	**abgeben** äp'gābən
unleaded	**bleifrei** blī'frī
valve	**das Ventil** däs ventēl'
vehicle registration	**der Kfz-Schein** dār kä`-ef-tset'-shīn
warning triangle	**das Warndreieck** däs värn'drī`ek
wheel	**das Rad** däs rät
windshield washer	**die Scheibenwaschanlage** dē
	shī'bənväsh-änlä`gə
windshield wiper	**der Scheibenwischer** dār shī'bənvishər
wiper blades	**die Scheibenwischerblätter** *(plural)*
	dē shī'bənvishərblet`ər
witness	**der Zeuge** dār tsoi'gə

BUS, SUBWAY, TAXI

By Bus and Subway

Where's the nearest subway station?	**Wo ist die nächste U-Bahn-Station?** vō ist dē nā<u>sh</u>s'tə ōō'-bän-sht<u>ä</u>tsyōn'?
Where does the *bus/streetcar* to … stop?	**Wo hält *der Bus/die Straßenbahn* nach …?** vō helt *dār bōōs/dē shträ'sənbän* nä<u>h</u> …?
Which *bus/train* goes to …?	***Welcher Bus/Welche Bahn* fährt nach …?** vel'<u>sh</u>ər bōōs/vel'<u>sh</u>ə bän färt nä<u>h</u> …?

> **!** **Die Linie …** dē lē'nē·ə   The …

When is the next *bus/train* to …?	**Wann fährt der nächste *Bus/Zug* nach …?** v<u>ä</u>n färt dār nā<u>sh</u>s'tə *bōōs/tsōōk* nä<u>h</u> …?
Does this *bus/train* go to …?	**Fährt dieser *Bus/Zug* nach …?** färt dē'zər *bōōs/dtsōōk* nä<u>h</u> …?
Do I have to change for …?	**Muss ich nach … umsteigen?** mōōs i<u>sh</u> nä<u>h</u> … ōōm'shtīgən?
Could you tell me where I have to *get off/change*, please?	**Sagen Sie mir bitte, wo ich *aussteigen/umsteigen* muss?** zä'gən zē mēr bit'ə, vō i<u>sh</u> ous'shtīgən/ōōm'shtīgən mōōs?

3

| Where can I buy a ticket? | **Wo gibt es die Fahrscheine?** |
| | vō gēpt es dē fär'shīnə? |

| I'd like a ticket to ..., please. | **Bitte einen Fahrschein nach ...** |
| | bit'ə i'nən fär'shīn näh ... |

| Are there ... | **Gibt es ...** gēpt es ... |

day passes?	**Tageskarten?** tä'gəskärtən?
multiple-ride tickets?	**Mehrfahrtenkarten?**
	mār'färtən·kär'tən?
weekly tickets?	**Wochenkarten?** vôh'ən·kär'tən?

Taxi!

| Could you order a taxi for me for ...? | **Könnten Sie für ... Uhr ein Taxi für mich bestellen?** ken'tən zē fēr ... ōōr in täk'sē fēr mish bəshtel'ən? |

| How much is it to ...? | **Wie viel kostet es nach ...?** vē fēl kôs'tət es näh ...? |

| Could you take me ..., please? | **Bitte ...** bit'ə ... |

to the airport	**zum Flughafen!** tsōōm flōōk'häfən!
to the ... Hotel	**zum Hotel ...!** tsōōm hôtel'...!
downtown	**in die Innenstadt!** in dē in'ənshtät!
to ... *Street/Road*	**in die ... Straße!** in dē ... shträ'sə!

Could you *wait/stop* here (for a minute), please?

Warten/Halten Sie hier bitte (einen Augenblick)! vär'tən/häl'tən zē hēr bit'ə (i'nən ougənblik')!

Bus, Rail, Taxi

bus	**der Bus** dār bōōs
cab	**das Taxi** däs täk'sē
to change	**umsteigen** ōōm'shtigən
downtown	**das Stadtzentrum** däs shtät'tsen`trōōm
day pass	**die Tageskarte** dē tä'gəskärtə
direction	**die Richtung** dē rish'tōōng
driver	**der Fahrer** dār fä'rər
end of the line	**die Endstation** dē ent'shtätsyōn`
fare	**der Fahrpreis** dār fär'prīs
inspector	**der Kontrolleur** dār kôntrôlär'
receipt	**die Quittung** dē kvit'ōōng
schedule	**der Fahrplan** dār fär'plän
stop	**die Haltestelle** dē häl'təshtelə
to stop	**halten** häl'tən
subway	**die U-Bahn** dē ōō'-bän
taxi	**das Taxi** däs täk'sē
taxi stand	**der Taxistand** dār täk'sēshtänt
terminal	**der Busbahnhof** dār bōōs'bän`hōf
ticket	**die Fahrkarte** dē fär'kärtə

3

| ticket (vending) machine | **der Fahrkartenautomat** dār fär'kärtənoutōmät' |
| weekly ticket | **die Wochenkarte** dē vôh'ənkärtə |

Hitchhiking

I'm on my way to ...	**Ich möchte nach ...** i_sh_ me_sh_'tə näh ...
Where are you going?	**Wohin fahren Sie?** vō'hin fä'rən zē?
Could you give me a ride (as far as ...)?	**Können Sie mich (bis ...) mitnehmen?** ken'ən zē mi_sh_ (bis ...) mit'nāmən?

| **Wo wollen Sie aussteigen?** vō vôl'ən zē ous'shtīgən? | Where do you want to get out? |

| Could you let me out here, please? | **Können Sie mich hier bitte aussteigen lassen?** ken'ən zē mi_sh_ hēr bit'ə ous'shtīgən läs'ən? |
| Thanks for the lift. | **Vielen Dank fürs Mitnehmen.** fē'lən dängk fērs mit'nāmən. |

Food and Drink

SPEISEKARTE MENU

Suppen, Salate Soups, Salads
und Vorspeisen and Appetizers

die Artischocken *(plural)* artichokes
dē är'tēshôk'ən

die Bohnensuppe dē bean soup
bō'nənzoōpə

die Champignoncremesuppe cream of mushroom soup
dē shäm'pinyôN·krām`zoōpə

die Erbsensuppe dē split pea soup
erp'sənzoōpə

die Fischsuppe dē fish'soōpə fish soup

die Fleischbrühe dē flīsh'brē·ə bouillon

    mit Ei mit ī with egg

    mit Fleischeinlage with meat
    mit flīsh'inlä`gə

    mit Nudeln mit noō'dəln with vermicelli

    mit Reis mit rīs with rice

der Geflügelsalat chicken salad
där gəflē'gəlzälät'

der gemischte Salat chef salad
där gəmish'tə zälät'

die Gemüsesuppe vegetable soup
dē gəmē'zəzoōpə

94

der geräucherte Lachs	smoked salmon
dār gəroi'shərtə läks	
der griechische Salat	Greek salad
dār grē'shishə zälät'	
die Grießnockerlsuppe	semolina-dumpling soup
dē grēs'nôkərlzōōp`ə	
der grüne Salat	green salad
dār grē̠'nə zälät'	
der Heringstopf	herring salad
dār hā'rings·tôpf	
die Hühnerbrühe	chicken broth
dē hē̠'nərbrē̠·ə	
die Hühnercremesuppe	cream of chicken soup
dē hē̠'nərkrāmzōōp`ə	
die Hummersuppe	lobster soup
dē hōōm'ərzōōpə	
die Kartoffelsuppe	potato soup
dē kärtôf'əlzōōpə	
die klare Suppe	consommé
dē klä'rə zōōp`ə	
die Königinpastetchen	vol au vents with a poultry
(plural) dē kȩ̈'niginpästā`tshən	filling
der Krabbencocktail	prawn cocktail
dār kräb'ənkôk`tāl	
die Lauchsuppe	leek soup
dē louh̠'zōōpə	

4

die Leberknödelsuppe	liver-dumpling soup
dē lā'bərknȫdəlzōōp`ə	
die Linsensuppe	lentil soup
dē lin'zənzōōpə	
die Melone dē məlō'nə	melon
die Ochsenschwanzsuppe	oxtail soup
dē ôk'sənshväntsōōp`ə	
der Parmaschinken	Parma ham
dār pär'mäshing`kən	
der Räucheraal dār roi'shəräl`	smoked eel
der Räucherlachs	smoked salmon
dār roi'shərläks`	
die Schildkrötensuppe	turtle soup
dē shilt'krātənzōōp`ə	
die Schnecken *(plural)*	escargots
dē shnek'ən	
die Spargelcremesuppe	cream of asparagus soup
dē shpär'gəlkrāmzōōp`ə	
die Tagessuppe	today's soup
dē tä'gəsōōpə	
die Tomatensuppe	tomato soup
dē tōmä'tənzōōpə	
die Weinbergschnecken	escargots
(plural) dē vīn'bärkshnek`ən	
die Zwiebelsuppe	French onion soup
dē tsvē'bəlzōōpə	

Frühstück *Breakfast*

das Brot däs brōt — bread

das Brötchen däs brāt'shən — roll, bun

die Butter dē bōōt'ər — butter

die Eier *(plural)* dē i'ər — eggs

der Früchtetee dār frish'tətā — fruit tea

die gekochten Eier *(plural)* dē gəkôh'tən i'ər — boiled eggs

der Grapefruitsaft dār grāp'frōōtsäft — grapefruit juice

der Honig dār hō'nish — honey

das Hörnchen däs hern'shən — crescent roll

der Joghurt dār yō'gōōrt — yogurt

der Kaffee dār käf'ā — coffee

der Kakao dār käkou' — cocoa

der Käse dār kā'zə — cheese

das Knäckebrot däs knek'əbrōt — crispbread, knäckebröd

die Margarine dē märgärē'nə — margarine

die Marmelade dē märməlä'də — jam

die Milch dē milsh — milk

das Müsli däs mēs'lē — granola

der Orangensaft dār ōräN'zhənzäft — orange juice

4

die pochierten Eier *(plural)*	poached eggs
dē pôshēr'tən l'ər	
der Quark dār kvärk	quark, cottage cheese
die Rühreier *(plural)*	scrambled eggs
dē rēr'ī-ər	
der Schinken dār shing'kən	ham
die Semmel dē zem'əl	roll, bun
die Spiegeleier *(plural)*	fried eggs sunnyside up
dē shpē'gəli·ər	
der Tee dār tā	tea
das Vollkornbrot	wholemeal bread
däs fôl'kôrnbrōt	
das Weißbrot däs vīs'brōt	white bread
die Wurst dē vŏŏrst	sausage

Fleischgerichte *Meat Dishes*

das Beefsteak däs bēf'stāk	beefsteak
die Bratwurst dē brät'vŏŏrst	fried sausage
die Bulette dē bŏŏlet'ə	meat patty
das Deutsche Beefsteak	beef patty
däs doit'shə bēf'stāk	
der falsche Hase	meatloaf
dār fäl'shə hä'zə	
das Faschierte däs fäshēr'tə	ground meat

das faschierte Laiberl	meat patty
däs fäshēr'tə lī'berl	
das Filetsteak däs filā'stäk	fillet steak
das Fleischpflanzerl	meat patty, hamburger
däs flīsh'pfläntsərl	
die Frikadelle dē frikädel'ə	meat patty, hamburger
das Gulasch däs gōō'läsh	goulash
das Hackfleisch däs häk'flīsh	ground meat
das Hammelfleisch	mutton
däs häm'əlflīsh	
der Hase dār hä'zə	rabbit
der Hirsch dār hirsh	venison
das Kalbfleisch däs kälp'flīsh	veal
der Kalbsbraten	roast veal
dār kälps'brätən	
das Kalbsschnitzel	veal cutlet
däs kälps'shnitsəl	
das Kaninchen	rabbit
däs känēn'shən	
das Kasseler Ripperl	smoked pork chop
däs käs'ələr rīp'ərl	
das Kotelett däs kôtlet'	chop, cutlet
die Lammkeule dē läm'koilə	leg of lamb
das Lammkotelett	lamb chop
däs läm'kôtlet'	

4

das Lendensteak	tenderloin steak
däs len'dənstäk	
das Ragout däs rägōō'	stew
das Reh däs rā	venison
das Rostbratwürstchen	fried/grilled sausage
däs rôst'brätvjrst'shən	
die Roulade dē rōōlä'də	roulade, roll
das Rumpsteak	rumpsteak
däs rōōmp'stäk	
der Sauerbraten	sour roast
där zou'ərbrätən	
der Schweinebraten	roast pork
där shvī'nəbrätən	
das Schweinekotelett	pork chop
däs shvī'nəkôtlet'	
die Schweinshaxe	leg of pork
dē shvīns'häksə	
das Wiener Würstchen	frankfurter, wiener
däs vē'nər vjrst'shən	
das Wiener Schnitzel	Wiener schnitzel,
däs vē'nər shnit'səl	breaded veal escalope
das Wild däs vilt	game
das Würstchen	sausage
däs vjrst'shən	
der Zwiebelrostbraten	steak and onion
där tsvē'bəlrôstbrätən	

Geflügel *Fowl/Poultry*

das Backhendl däs bäk'hendəl   deep-fried chicken

das Brathähnchen   roast chicken
däs brät'hänshən

die Ente dē en'tə   duck

der Fasan där fäzän'   pheasant

der Gänsebraten   roast goose
där gen'zəbrätən

die Gänsekeule   leg of goose
dē gen'zəkoilə

das Hähnchen däs hän'shən   chicken

    das gebackene -   baked chicken
    däs gəbäk'ənə hän'shən

die Hähnchenbrust   breast of chicken
dē hän'shənbrōōst

die Hähnchenkeule   chicken leg
dē hän'shənkoilə

der Truthahn där trōōt'hän   turkey

4

Fisch und Meeresfrüchte *Fish and Seafood*

der Barsch där bärsh   perch

die Forelle dē förel'ə   trout

die Garnelen *(plural)*   shrimps
dē gärnä'lən

der Heilbutt där hīl'bōōt   halibut

der Hering dār hā'ring	herring
der Hummer dār hōōm'ər	lobster
der Kabeljau dār kä'bəlyou	cod
die Krabben *(plural)*	prawns
dē kräb'ən	
der Lachs dār läks	salmon
die Makrele dē mäkrā'lə	mackerel
die Miesmuscheln *(plural)*	mussels
dē mēs'mōōshəln	
die Muscheln *(plural)*	scallops
dē mōōsh'əln	
der Schwertfisch	swordfish
dār shvärt'fish	
der Seelachs dār zā'läks	saithe
das Seezungenfilet	fillet of sole
däs zā'tsōōngənfilā	
der Steinbutt dār shtīn'bōōt	turbot
der Zander dār tsän'dər	perch-pike

Nudeln und Klöße   *Pasta and Dumplings*

die Bandnudeln *(plural)*	tagliatelle
dē bänt'nōōdəln	
die Fadennudeln *(plural)*	vermicelli
dē fä'dənōōdəln	
die Kartoffelklöße *(plural)*	potato dumplings
dē kärtôf'əlklāsə	

102

die Makkaroni *(plural)*	maccaroni
dē mäkärō'nē	
die Maultaschen *(plural)*	ravioli
dē moul'täshən	
die Nudeln *(plural)*	pasta
dē nōō'dəln	
die Semmelknödel *(plural)*	bread dumplings
dē zem'əlknādəl	
die Teigwaren *(plural)*	pasta
dē tīk'värən	
die Spätzle *(plural)*	spätzle noodles
dē shpets'lə	
die Spaghetti *(plural)*	spaghetti
dē shpäget'ē	

Gemüse und Beilagen   *Vegetables and Side Dishes*

der Blumenkohl	cauliflower
där blōō'mənkōl	
die Champignons *(plural)*	mushrooms
dē shäm'pinyôNs	
der Eissalat där īs'älät	iceberg lettuce
der Endiviensalat	chicory crown
där endē'vē·ənzälät	
die Erbsen *(plural)* dē erp'sən	peas
die Folienkartoffel	baked potato
dē fō'lē·ənkärtôf əl	

4

die grünen Bohnen *(plural)*	green beans
dē grȳ'nən bō'nən	
der Grünkohl dār grȳn'kōl	kale
die Gurke dē gōōr'kə	cucumber
die Karotten *(plural)*	carrots
dē kärôt'ən	
das Kartoffelgratin	potatoes au gratin
däs kärtôf'əlgräteN'	
die Kartoffelpfannkuchen	potato pancakes
(plural) dē kärtôf'əlpfän'kōōhən	
das Kartoffelpüree	mashed potatoes
däs kärtôf'əlpērä	
der Kartoffelsalat	potato salad
dār kärtôf'əlzälät	
der Kohl dār kōl	cabbage
das Kraut däs krout	cabbage
der Krautsalat dār krout'sälät	coleslaw
die Linsen *(plural)* dē lin'zən	lentils
der Paprika dār päp'rikä	pepper
die Pilze *(plural)* dē pil'tsə	mushrooms
die Pommes frites *(plural)*	French fries
dē pôm frit'	
der Reis dār rīs	rice
der Rosenkohl dār rō'zənkōl	Brussels sprout
die Rote Bete dē rō'tə bā'tə	beetroot
der Rotkohl dār rōt'kōl	red cabbage

die Salzkartoffeln *(plural)*	boiled potatoes
dē zälts'kärtôf əln	
das Sauerkraut	sauerkraut
däs zou'ərkrout	
die Schalotten *(plural)*	shallots
dē shälôt'ən	
der Spargel dār shpär'gəl	asparagus
die Spargelspitzen *(plural)*	asparagus tips
dē shpär'gəlshpitsən	
der Spinat dār shpinät'	spinach
die Tomate dē tōmä'tə	tomato
der Wirsing(kohl)	savoy cabbage
dār vir'sing(kōl)	
die Zwiebel dē tsvē'bəl	onion

Kräuter und Gewürze *Herbs and Spices*

das Basilikum däs bäzē'likōom	basil
der Estragon dār es'trägôn	tarragon
die Kapern *(plural)* dē kä'pərn	capers
der Knoblauch dār knōp'louh	garlic
der Kren dār krān	horseradish
der Kümmel dār kim'əl	caraway seed
der Meerrettich dār mār'etish	horseradish
der Muskat dār mōōskät'	nutmeg
der Pfeffer dār pfef'ər	pepper

4

der Rosmarin dār rōs'märēn	rosemary
das Salz däs zälts	salt
der Schnittlauch	chives
dār shnit'lou̱ẖ	
der Senf dār zenf	mustard
der Thymian dār tḡ'mē-än	thyme
der Zimt dār tsimt	cinnamon

Zubereitungsarten *Methods of Preparation*

durch(gebraten)	well done
dōōr̲s̲h̲'gəbrätən	
eingelegt in'gəläkt	pickled
englisch eng'lish	rare
filetiert filätērt'	filleted
frittiert fritērt'	deep-fried
gebacken gəbäk'ən	baked
(auf dem Rost) **gebraten**	broiled
(ouf däm rôst) gəbrä'tən	
(in der Pfanne) **gebraten**	fried
(in dār pfän'ə) gəbrä'tən	
gegrillt gəgrilt'	grilled, barbecued
gekocht gəkô̱ẖt'	boiled
geräuchert gəroi's̲h̲ərt	smoked
geschmort gəshmört'	braised
... gratin ō gräteN'	au gratin

106

mariniert märinērt'	marinated
medium mā'dē·ōōm	medium(-rare)
pochiert pôshērt'	poached

Käse *Cheese*

der Blauschimmelkäse där blou'shiməlkā'zə	blue cheese
der Camembert där kä'məNbär	camembert
der Edamer där ä'dämər	edam
der Emmentaler där em'əntälər	Swiss cheese
der Frischkäse där frish'kāzə	cream cheese
der Gouda där gou'dä	gouda
der Hüttenkäse där hit'ənkäzə	cottage cheese
der Parmesan där pärmezän'	parmesan cheese
der Schafskäse där shäfs'käzə	feta cheese
der Ziegenkäse där tsē'gənkäzə	goat's cheese

4

Nachspeisen *Desserts*

der Apfelkuchen där äp'fəlkōōhən	apple pie
das Eis däs īs	ice cream

der Karamellpudding	caramel custard
dār kärämel'pōoding	
das Kompott däs kômpôt'	stewed fruit
der Obstsalat dār ōpst'sälät	fruit salad
die Obsttorte dē ōps'tôrtə	fruit flan
die Palatschinken *(plural)*	stuffed pancakes
dē pälät·shing'kən	
die Rote Grütze dē rō'tə grit'sə	summer berries
die Sachertorte dē zäh'ərtôrtə	sacher cake
die Schokoladentorte	chocolate cake
dē shōkōlä'dəntôr'tə	
der Schokoladenpudding	chocolate pudding
dār shōkōlä'dənpōoding	
die Schwarzwälder Kirsch-	Black Forest gâteau
torte dē shvärts'veldər	
kirsh'tôrtə	
die Vanillecreme	custard
dē vänil'yəkräm	
der Vanillepudding	vanilla pudding
dār vänil'yəpōoding	

Obst Fruit

die Ananas dē än'änäs	pineapple
der Apfel dār äp'fəl	apple
die Aprikose dē äprikō'zə	apricot

108

die Banane dē bänä'nə	banana	
die Birne dē bir'nə	pear	
die Erdbeeren *(plural)*	strawberries	
dē ärt'bärən		
die Heidelbeeren *(plural)*	blueberries	
dē hī'dəlbärən		
die Himbeeren *(plural)*	raspberries	
dē him'bärən		
die Kirschen *(plural)*	cherries	
dē kir'shən		
die Mandarine	tangerine	
dē mändärē'nə		
die Orange dē ôräN'zhə	orange	
der Pfirsich där pfir'zish	peach	
die Pflaume dē pflou'mə	plum	
die Weintrauben *(plural)*	grapes	
dē vīn'troubən		

GETRÄNKE BEVERAGES

4

Wein, Champagner   *Wine, Champagne*
und Sekt   *and Sparkling Wine*

der Apfelwein där äp'fəlvīn   cider
der Burgunder   Burgundy
där bŏŏrgŏŏn'dər

der Champagner	champagne
där shämpän'yər	
der Frankenwein	Franconian wine
där fräng'kənvīn	
der Glühwein där glē'vīn	mulled wine
der Hauswein där hous'vīn	house wine
der Moselwein där mō'zəlvīn	Moselle wine
der offene Wein där ôf'ənə vīn	wine by the glass
der Portwein där pôrt'vīn	port
der Rheinwein där rīn'vīn	Rhine wine
der Rosé där rōzā'	rosé
der Rotwein där rōt'vīn	red wine
der Schaumwein	sparkling wine
där shoum'vīn	
der Sekt där zekt	sparkling wine
süß zēs	sweet
trocken trôk'ən	dry
der Wein där vīn	wine
der Weißwein där vīs'vīn	white wine

Bier *Beer*

das alkoholfreie Bier	non-alcoholic beer
däs äl'kōhôlfrī'ə bēr	
das Bier vom Fass	draft beer
däs bēr fôm fäs	

das Bockbier däs bôk'bēr	bock (beer)
das helle Bier däs hel'ə bēr	lager
das Pils däs pils	pils (beer)
das Starkbier däs shtärk'bēr	strong ale, stout
das Weißbier, das Weizenbier	weiss beer
däs vīs'bēr, däs vī'tsənbēr	

Andere alkoholische   *Other Alcoholic Drinks*
Getränke

der Gin dār jin	gin
der Grog dār grôk	grog, toddy
der Likör dār likār'	liqueur
der Magenbitter	cordial, herbal liqueur
dār mä'gənbit'ər	
der Punsch dār pōōnsh	punch
der Rum dār rōōm	rum
der Schnaps dār shnäps	spirits, hard liquor
der Weinbrand dār vīn'bränt	brandy
der Whiskey dār vis'kē	whiskey
der Wodka dār vôt'kä	vodka

4

Alkoholfreie Getränke   *Non-alcoholic Drinks*

das alkoholfreie Getränk	soft drink
däs äl'kōhōlfrī'ə gətrengk'	
der Apfelsaft dār äp'fəlzäft	apple juice

111

der Eiskaffee dār īs'kǎfā iced coffee

der Eistee dār īs'tā iced tea

das Leitungswasser tap water
dǎs lī'tōōngsvǎs'ər

die Limonade dē limōnä'də soda pop

das Milchmixgetränk milkshake
dǎs milsh'miksgətrengk`

das Mineralwasser mineral water
dǎs minərǎl'väsər

   mit Kohlensäure carbonated
   mit kō'lənzoirə

   ohne Kohlensäure non-carbonated
   ō'nə kō'lənzoirə

der Obstsaft dār ōpst'säft fruit juice

der Saft dār zäft juice

das Selterswasser club soda
dǎs zel'tərsväsər

das Tonic dǎs tôn'ik tonic water

die Zitronenlimonade lemon soda
dē tsitrō'nənlimōnä'də

Heiße Getränke   *Hot Drinks*

der Kaffee dār kǎf'ā coffee

   mit Milch und/oder Zucker with milk and/or sugar
   mit milsh ōōnt/ō'dər tsōōk'ər

112

schwarz shvärts		black
der Kakao dār käkou'		cocoa
der Kräutertee dār kroi'tərtā		herbal tea
die Schokolade dē shōkōlä'də		hot chocolate
der Tee dār tā		tea
mit Zitrone mit tsitrō'nə		with lemon

INFORMATION

Is there … near here?	**Wo gibt es hier …** vō gēpt es hēr …
a café	**ein Café?** in käfā'?
a bar	**eine Kneipe?** i'nə knī'pə?
a good/an inexpensive restaurant	**ein gutes/preiswertes Restaurant?** in gōō'təs/prīs'vārtəs restôräN'?
A table for …, please.	**Einen Tisch für … Personen bitte.** i'nən tish fēr … pərzō'nən, bit'ə.
Is this seat taken?	**Ist dieser Platz noch frei?** ist dē'zər pläts nôh frī?
Do you have a highchair?	**Haben Sie einen Hochstuhl?** hä'bən zē i'nən hōh'shtōōl?

4

113

Excuse me, where are the rest rooms?	**Entschuldigung, wo sind hier die Toiletten?** entshōōl'digōōng, vō zint hēr dē tô-älet'ən?

! **Hier entlang.** hēr entläng'. (Right) This way.

WAITER!

May I see the *menu/ wine list*, please?	**Die *Karte/Getränkekarte*, bitte.** dē *kär'tə/gətreng'kəkärtə*, bit'ə.
Are you still serving hot meals?	**Gibt es jetzt noch etwas Warmes zu essen?** gēpt es yetst nôh et'väs vär'məs tsōō es'ən?
I just want something to drink.	**Ich möchte nur etwas trinken.** ish mesh'tə nōōr et'väs tring'kən.

? **Was möchten Sie trinken?** vas mesh'tən zē tring'kən?	What would you like to drink?

I'd like ..., please.	**Ich möchte ...** ish mēshtə ...
a glass of *red wine/ white wine*	**ein Glas *Rotwein/Weißwein*.** īn gläs rōt'vīn/vīs'vīn.
a beer	**ein Bier.** īn bēr.

a *small/large* bottle of mineral water	**eine *kleine/große* Flasche Mineralwasser.** ī'nə *klī'nə/grō'sə* fläsh'ə minəräl'väsər.	
a cup of coffee	**eine Tasse Kaffee.** ī'nə täs'ə käf'ā.	

? **Was möchten Sie essen?**
● väs mesh'tən zē es'ən?

What would you like to eat?

I'd like …	**Ich möchte …** ish mesh'tə …

What would you recommend?	**Was empfehlen Sie mir?** väs empfā'lən zē mēr?

! **Ich empfehle Ihnen …**
● ish empfā'lə ē'nən …

I can recommend …

Do you have any regional specialties?	**Haben Sie Spezialitäten aus der Region?** hä'bən zē shpetsyälitä'tən ous dār rāgyōn'?

Do you have children's portions?	**Haben Sie Kinderteller?** hä'bən zē kin'dərtelər?

Do you serve …	**Haben Sie …** hä'bən zē …
diabetic meals?	**diabetische Kost?** dē·äbā'tishə kôst?
low fat/dietary meals?	**Diätkost?** dē·āt'kôst?
vegetarian dishes?	**vegetarische Gerichte?** vāgātä'rishə gərish'tə?

4

115

Does it have …? I'm not allowed to eat *that/them/it*.	**Ist … in dem Gericht? Ich darf das nicht essen.** ist … in dām gərisht? ish därf däs nisht es'ən.	

? Was nehmen Sie als *Vorspeise/ Nachtisch*? väs nā'mən zē äls fōr'shpīzə/näḥ'tish?

What would you like for *an appetizer/ dessert*?

No, thank you, I don't care for *an appetizer/ any dessert*.
Danke, ich nehme *keine Vorspeise/ keinen Nachtisch*. däng'kə, ish nā'mə kī'nə fōr'shpīze/kī'nən näḥ'tish.

? Welche Salatsoße hätten Sie gern? vel'shə zälät'sōsə het'ən zē gern?

What sort of salad dressing would you like?

Could I have … instead of …?
Könnte ich … statt … haben? kən'tə ish … shtät … hä'bən?

? Wie möchten Sie Ihr Steak? vē meshʹtən zē ēr stāk?

How would you like your steak?

Rare.	**Blutig.** blōō'tish.
Medium rare.	**Englisch.** eng'lish.
Medium.	**Medium.** mā'dē-ōōm.
Well done.	**Gut durchgebraten.** gōōt dōōrsh'gəbrätən.

| Could you bring me another ..., please? | **Bitte bringen Sie mir noch (*ein/eine/einen*) ...** bit'ə bring'ən zē mēr nô<u>h</u> (*īn, i'nə, i'nən*) ... |

COMPLAINTS

I didn't order this. I asked for...	**Das habe ich nicht bestellt. Ich wollte ...** däs hä'bə i<u>sh</u> ni<u>sh</u>t bəshtelt'. i<u>sh</u> vôl'tə ...
The ... *is/are* missing.	**Hier *fehlt/fehlen* noch ...** hēr fālt/fā'lən nô<u>h</u> ...
The food is *cold/too salty*.	**Das Essen ist *kalt/versalzen*.** däs es'ən ist <u>k</u>ält/ferzäl'tsən.
The meat hasn't been cooked long enough.	**Das Fleisch ist nicht lang genug gebraten.** däs flīsh ist ni<u>sh</u>t läng gənōōk' gəbrä'tən.
The meat is tough.	**Das Fleisch ist zäh.** däs flīsh ist tsā.
Could you take it back, please?	**Bitte nehmen Sie es zurück.** bit'ə nā'mən zē es tsōōrik'.

4

THE CHECK, PLEASE.

Could I have the check, please?	**Ich möchte zahlen.** <u>ish</u> m<u>e</u>sh'tə tsä'lən.
I'd like a receipt.	**Ich möchte eine Quittung.** <u>ish</u> m<u>e</u>sh'tə i'nə kvit͞o͞ong.
We'd like separate checks, please.	**Wir möchten getrennt bezahlen.** vēr m<u>e</u>sh'tən gətrent' bətsä'lən.
I'd like to pay for your meal.	**Darf ich *Sie/dich* einladen?** därf i<u>sh</u> zē/di<u>sh</u> in'lädən?
You're my guest today.	***Sie sind/Du bist* heute mein Gast.** zē zint/d͞o͞o bist hoi'tə mīn gäst.

❓ Hat es Ihnen geschmeckt?
hät es ē'nən gəshmekt'?

Did you enjoy your meal?

It was very nice, thank you.

Danke, sehr gut. däng'kə, zār g͞o͞ot.

INFO Unlike in the USA there are no hard and fast rules for tipping. As a general guide, if you are satisfied with the service and the food, you merely generously round up the check as a tip. For example, if your check comes to 8.70 round it up to 10 DM. If it is about 46.50 make it 50 DM. If you often dine at the same place it is advisable to be a little more generous when tipping as you will be rewarded with better service.

118

DINING WITH FRIENDS

Cheers! **Zum Wohl!** tsōōm vol!

? **Wie schmeckt es *Ihnen/dir*?** How are you
vē shmekt es ē'nən/dēr? enjoying your meal?

It's very good, thank **Danke, sehr gut.** däng'kə, zār gōōt.
you.

? **Noch etwas …?** nôh et'väs …? Would you like some
more?

Yes, please. **Ja, gerne.** yä, ger'nə.

No thank you, I'm full. **Danke, ich bin satt.** däng'kə, ish bin
zät.

Would you pass me ***Würden Sie/Würdest du* mir bitte …**
the …, please? **reichen?** vir'dən zē/vir'dəst dōō mēr
bit'ə … rī'shən?

I don't care for/I'm **Ich *möchte/darf* keinen Alkohol**
not allowed to have **trinken.** ish mesh'tə/därf kī'nən
alcohol. äl'kōhōl tring'kən.

Do you mind if **Stört es *Sie/dich*, wenn ich rauche?**
I smoke? shtārt es zē/dish, ven ish rou'hə?

4

119

INFO In more luxurious restaurants it is advisable to book a table well in advance, especially for the evening. Then, when you arrive, you only have to give your name and the head waiter will show you to your table. In everyday and simple eateries you don't need to book a table. You just choose a free table.

Food and Drink

ashtray	**der Aschenbecher** där äsh'ənbe<u>sh</u>ər
bar	**die Kneipe** dē knī'pə
to be full	**satt sein** zät zīn
to be hungry	**hungrig sein** hŏŏng'rish zīn
to be thirsty	**durstig sein** dŏŏrs'ti<u>sh</u> zīn
bone	*(meat)* **der Knochen;** *(fish)* **die Gräte** där knô<u>h</u>'ən, dē grä'tə
bottle	**die Flasche** dē fläsh'ə
black coffee	**der schwarze Kaffee** där shvär'tsə käf'ā
bread	**das Brot** däs brōt
breakfast	**das Frühstück** däs frē'shtik
to bring	**bringen** bring'ən
butter	**die Butter** dē bŏŏt'ər
cake	**der Kuchen** där kōō'hən
carafe	**die Karaffe** dē käräf'ə
chamomile tea	**der Kamillentee** där kämil'əntā

120

cheese	**der Käse** dār kā'zə
cocoa	**der Kakao** dār kạkou'
coffee	**der Kaffee** dār kạf'ā
coffee with cream	**der Kaffee mit Sahne** dār kạf'ā mit zä'nə
coffee with sugar	**der Kaffee mit Zucker** dār kạf'ā mit tsōōk'ər
course	**der Gang** dār gạng
crudités	**die Rohkost** dē rō'kôst
cup	**die Tasse** dē tạs'ə
cutlery	**das Besteck** dạs bəshtek'
decaffeinated coffee, decaf	**der koffeinfreie Kaffee** dār kôf·ā·ēn'frī·ə kạf'ā
dessert	**der Nachtisch** dār näḫ'tish
diabetic	**der Diabetiker, die Diabetikerin** dār dē·äbā'tikər, dē dē·äbā'tikərin
diabetic	**diabetisch** dē·äbā'tish
diet	**die Diät** dē dē·āt'
dinner	**das Abendessen** dạs ä'bənt·es·ən
dish of the day	**das Tagesgericht** dạs tä'gəsgərisht
drink	**das Getränk** dạs gətrengk'
to drink	**trinken** tring'kən
to eat	**essen** es'ən
fat	**das Fett** dạs fet
filling	**die Füllung** dē fịl'ōōng
fish	**der Fisch** dār fish

4

food	**das Essen** däs es'ən
fork	**die Gabel** dē gä'bəl
fresh	**frisch** frish
fried egg sunny-side up	**das Spiegelei** däs shpē'gəl·ī
fruit	**das Obst** däs ōpst
garlic	**der Knoblauch** dār knōp'lou<u>h</u>
glass	**das Glas** däs gläs
greasy	**fett** fet
ham	**der Schinken** dār shing'kən
hard	**hart** härt
honey	**der Honig** dār hō'ni<u>sh</u>
hot	**scharf** shärf
ice	**das Eis** däs īs
ice cubes	**die Eiswürfel** *(plural)* dē īs'vērfəl
jam	**die Marmelade** dē märməlä'də
knife	**das Messer** däs mes'ər
lean	**mager** mä'gər
lettuce	**der Kopfsalat** dār kôpf'sälät
light food	**die Schonkost** dē shōn'kôst
lunch	**das Mittagessen** däs mit'äg·es`ən
main course	**das Hauptgericht** däs houpt'gəri<u>sh</u>t
margarine	**die Margarine** dē märgärē'nə
mayonnaise	**die Mayonnaise** dē mäyōnā'zə
meal	**das Gericht** däs gəri<u>sh</u>t'
meat	**das Fleisch** däs flīsh

122

milk	**die Milch** dē milsh	
mineral water	**das Mineralwasser**	
	däs mēnəräl'väsər	
mushrooms	**die Pilze** *(plural)* dē pil'tsə	
mustard	**der Senf** dār zenf	
napkin	**die Serviette** dē zervē·et'ə	
non-alcoholic	**alkoholfrei** äl'kōhōlfrī	
oil	**das Öl** däs āl	
to order	**bestellen** bəshtel'ən	
to pay	**zahlen** tsä'lən	
to pay for *someone's*	*jemanden* **einladen** yā'mändən	
meal	in'lädən	
pepper	**der Pfeffer** dār pfef'ər	
piece	**das Stück** däs shtik	
plate	**der Teller** dār tel'ər	
portion	**die Portion** dē pôrtsyōn'	
rest room	**die Toilette** dē tô·älet'ə	
salad	**der Salat** dār zälät'	
salad dressing	**die Salatsoße** dē zälät'zōsə	
salt	**das Salz** däs sälts	
sauce	**die Soße** dē zō'sə	
scrambled egg	**das Rührei** däs rēr'ī	
seasoned	**gewürzt** gəvirtst'	
slice	**die Scheibe** dē shī'bə	
soup	**die Suppe** dē zōōp'ə	
sour	**sauer** zou'ər	

4

sparkling mineral water	**das Mineralwasser mit Kohlensäure** däs mēnəräl'väsər mit kō'lənzoirə
spice	**das Gewürz** däs gəvirts'
spoon	**der Löffel** dār lef'əl
sugar	**der Zucker** dār tsōōk'ər
supper	**das Abendessen** däs ä'bənte'sən
sweet	**süß** zēs
sweetener	**der Süßstoff** dār zēs'stöf
table	**der Tisch** dār tish
to taste	**schmecken** shmek'ən
tea	**der Tee** dār tā
teaspoon	**der Teelöffel** dār tā'lefəl
tip	**das Trinkgeld** däs tringk'gelt
toothpick	**der Zahnstocher** dār tsän'shtôhər
vegetables	**das Gemüse** däs gəmē'zə
vegetarian	**vegetarisch** vegətä'rish
vinegar	**der Essig** dār es'ih̲
waiter	**der Kellner** dār kel'nər
waitress	**die Kellnerin** dē kel'nərin
white bread	**das Weißbrot** däs vis'brōt

Sightseeing

TOURIST INFORMATION

INFO In towns and in many villages there are Tourist Information Bureaus which are easily recognizable by their sign, a fat red „i" with a large dot. They will provide you with details of accommodations and comprehensive information on local places of interest.

May I have …	**Ich möchte …** ish mesh'tə …
a map of the area?	**einen Plan von der Umgebung.** i'nən plän fôn dār ōōmgā'bōōng.
a map of the city?	**einen Stadtplan.** i'nən shtät'plän.
a current events guide?	**einen Veranstaltungskalender.** i'nən ferän'shtältōōngs·kälen'dər.
a list of hotels?	**ein Hotelverzeichnis.** i'n hōtel'fertsish'nis.
Are there *sightseeing tours/guided walking tours* of the city?	**Gibt es *Stadtrundfahrten/Stadtführungen*?** gēpt es shtät'rōōnt·fär'tən/shtät'fē'rōōngən?
What are some of the places of interest here?	**Welche Sehenswürdigkeiten gibt es hier?** vel'shə zā'ənsvirdishkī'tən gēpt es hēr?
I'd like to visit …	**Ich möchte … besichtigen.** ish mesh'tə … bəzish'tigən.

126

| When do we start? | **Wann geht es los?** vän gāt es lōs? |

| When do we get back? | **Wann kommen wir zurück?** vän kôm'ən vēr tsōōrįk'? |

SIGTSEEING, EXCURSIONS

| *When/How long* is ... open? | **Wann/Wie lange ist ... geöffnet?** vän/vē läng'ə ist ... ge-ęf'nət? |

| *What's the admission charge?/How much does the guided tour cost?* | **Wie viel kostet der Eintritt/die Führung?** vē fēl kôs'tət dār in'trit/ dē fē'rōōng? |

| Is there a discount for ... | **Gibt es eine Ermäßigung für ...** gēpt es i'nə ermä'sigōōng fēr ... |

families?	**Familien?** fämē'lē·ən?
children?	**Kinder?** kin'dər?
students?	**Studenten?** shtōōden'tən?

| **?** | **Haben Sie einen Ausweis dabei?** hä'bən zē i'nən ous'vīs däbī'? | Do you have your ID with you? |

| When does the guided tour begin? | **Wann beginnt die Führung?** vän bəgint' dē fē'rōōng? |

| *One ticket/Two tickets,* please. | **Eine Karte/Zwei Karten,** bitte. i'nə kär'tə/tsvī kär'tən, bit'ə. |

5

127

Two adults and two children, please.	**Zwei Erwachsene und zwei Kinder, bitte.** tsvī erväk'sənə ōōnt tsvī kin'dər, bit'ə.
Is *photography/video-taping* allowed?	**Darf man *fotografieren/filmen*?** därf män fōtōgräfē'rən/fil'mən?
What *building/monument* is that?	**Was für ein *Gebäude/Denkmal* ist das?** väs fēr īn gəboi'də/dengk'mäl ist däs?
Do you have a *catalog/guide*?	**Haben Sie einen *Katalog/Führer*?** hä'bən zē ī'nən kätälōg′/fē′rər?

INFO A practical way of exploring your holiday destination on your own in large cities is by buying a ticket for the public transport system (Hamburg-ticket, Vienna-ticket etc.). You can choose tickets which are valid for several days and these will enable you to travel as often as you like, and quite far into the suburbs as well, on any form of transport within the system without having to buy a new ticket each time.

Sightseeing, Excursions

admission	**der Eintritt** dār īn'trit
architect	**der Architekt** dār ärshitekt'
architecture	**die Architektur** dē är'shitektōōr'
art	**die Kunst** dē kōōnst

128

art collection	**die Gemäldesammlung** dē gəmäl´dəzäm˙loong
artist	**der Künstler** dār künst´lər
bell	**die Glocke** dē glôk´ə
botanical garden(s)	**der Botanische Garten** dār bōtä´nishə gär´tən
brewery	**die Brauerei** dē brou·ərī´
brochure	**der Prospekt** dār prôspekt´
bronze	**die Bronze** dē brôN´sə
building	**das Bauwerk** däs bou´värk
bust	**die Büste** dē büs´tə
catalog	**der Katalog** dār kätälōg´
cave	**die Höhle** dē hȫ´lə
ceiling	**die Decke** dē dek´ə
cemetery	**der Friedhof** dār frēt´hōf
century	**das Jahrhundert** däs yärhoon´dərt
ceramics	**die Keramik** dē kərä´mik
chapel	**die Kapelle** dē käpel´ə
church	**die Kirche** dē kir´shə
church service	**der Gottesdienst** dār gôt´əsdēnst
church tower	**der Kirchturm** dār kirsh´toorm
city hall	**das Rathaus** däs rät´hous
civil war	**der Bürgerkrieg** dār bir´gərkrēk
cliff	**die Klippe** dē klip´ə
closed	**geschlossen** gəshlôs´ən
conqueror	**der Eroberer** dār erō´bərər

5

cross	**das Kreuz** däs kroits
dam	**der Staudamm** där shtou'däm
discount	**die Ermäßigung** dē ermā'sigoong
discoverer	**der Entdecker** där entdek'ər
dome	**die Kuppel** dē koop'əl
downtown	**das Stadtzentrum** däs shtät'tsentroom
dune	**die Düne** dē dē̱'nə
early work	**das Frühwerk** däs frē̱'verk
era	**die Epoche** dē epôh'ə
etching	**die Radierung** dē rädē'roong
excavations	**die Ausgrabungen** *(plural)* dē ous'grä'boongən
excursion	**der Ausflug** där ous'floōk
exhibition	**die Ausstellung** dē ous'shteloong
Expressionism	**der Expressionismus** där ekspres'yōnis'moōs
façade	**die Fassade** dē fäsä'də
to film	**filmen** fil'mən
forest	**der Wald** där vält
fountain	**der Brunnen** där broōn'ən
fresco	**das Fresko** däs fres'kō
gallery	**die Galerie** dē gälərē'
garden	**der Garten** där gär'tən
gate	**das Tor** däs tōr
glass	**das Glas** däs gläs

130

grave	**das Grab** däs gräp
guided tour	**die Führung** dē f<u>ē</u>'rōōng
guided tour of the city	**die Stadtführung** dē shtät'fē̇rōōng
hall	**der Saal** där zäl
harbor	**der Hafen** där hä'fən
history	**die Geschichte** dē gəshish'tə
Impressionism	**der Impressionismus** där impres'yōnis'mōōs
inscription	**die Inschrift** dē in'shrift
lake	**der See** där zā
landscape	**die Landschaft** dē länt'shäft
late work	**das Spätwerk** däs shpāt'verk
library	**die Bibliothek** dē bēb'lē·ōtāk'
main entrance	**das Portal** däs pôrtäl'
map of the town	**der Stadtplan** där shtät'plän
marble	**der Marmor** där mär'mōr
memorial	**die Gedenkstätte** dē gədengk'shtetə
model	**das Modell** däs mōdel'
modern	**modern** mōdern'
monument	**das Denkmal** däs dengk'mäl
mosaic	**das Mosaik** däs mōzä·ik'
mountains	**das Gebirge** däs gəbir'gə
mural	**die Wandmalerei** dē vänt'mälərī'
museum	**das Museum** däs mōōzā'ōōm
national park	**der Nationalpark** där nä'tsyōnäl'pärk

5

nature preserve	**das Naturschutzgebiet** däs nätoor'shootsgəbēt
observatory	**die Sternwarte** dē shtern'värtə
oil painting	**die Ölmalerei** dē ȫl'mälərī'
open	**geöffnet** gə·ef'nət
opera (house)	**das Opernhaus** däs ō'pərnhous
organ	**die Orgel** dē ôr'gəl
original	**das Original** däs ōriginäl'
painter	**der Maler** där mä'lər
painting	**das Gemälde** däs gəmäl'də
painting	**die Malerei** dē mälərī'
park	**der Park** där pärk
part of the town	**der Stadtteil** där shtät'īl
pass	**der Pass** där päs
pedestrian zone	**die Fußgängerzone** dē foos'gengərtsō'nə
photo	**das Foto** däs fō'tō
picture	**das Bild** däs bilt
pillar	**die Säule** dē zoi'lə
planetarium	**das Planetarium** däs plä`nätär'ē·ōōm
portrait	**das Porträt** däs pôrtrā'
poster	**das Plakat** däs pläkät'
pottery	**die Töpferei** dē tepfərī'
print	**der Druck** där drook
to reconstruct	**rekonstruieren** räkônstroo·ē'rən
remains	**die Überreste** *(plural)* dē ē'bərestə

reservation	**das Reservat** däs räzervät'	
reservoir	**der Stausee** dār shtou'zā	
to restore	**restaurieren** restourē'rən	
river	**der Fluss** dār flōōs	
romantic	**romantisch** rōmän'tish	
roof	**das Dach** däs däh	
ruins	**die Ruinen** *(plural)* dē rōō·ē'nən	
sand	**der Sand** dār zänt	
sandstone	**der Sandstein** dār zänt'shtīn	
sculpture	**die Skulptur** dē skōōlptōōr'	
sights	**die Sehenswürdigkeiten** *(plural)* dē sā'ənsvirdishkī'tən	
sightseeing tour	**die Besichtigungsfahrt** dē bəzish'tigōōngsfärt	
slide	**das Dia** däs dē'ä	
square	**der Platz** dār pläts	
stalactite cave	**die Tropfsteinhöhle** dē trôpf'shtīnhȫ'lə	
statue	**die Statue** dē shtä'tōō·ə	
still life	**das Stillleben** däs shtil'ābən	
style	**der Stil** dār shtēl	
surrounding area	**die Umgebung** dē ōōmgā'bōōng	
synagogue	**die Synagoge** dē sinägō'gə	
to take photographs	**fotografieren** fōtōgräfē'rən	
theater	**das Theater** däs tā·ä'tər	
tour	**die Rundfahrt** dē rōōnt'färt	
tourist guide	**der Fremdenführer** dār frem'dənfē'rər	

5

tower	**der Turm** dār tōōrm
town	**die Stadt** dē shtät
town center	**das Stadtzentrum** däs shtät'tsentrōōm
university	**die Universität** dē ōō'nēverzētāt'
valley	**das Tal** däs täl
vase	**die Vase** dē vä'zə
view	**die Aussicht** dē ou'sisht
to visit	**besichtigen** bəzish'tigən
wall	**die Mauer** dē mou'ər
watercolor	**das Aquarell** däs äkvärel'
wood carving	**die Schnitzerei** dē shnitsərī'
zoo	**der Zoo** dār tsō

Animals

butterfly	**der Schmetterling** dār shmet'ərling
blackbird	**die Amsel** dē äm'zəl
cat	**die Katze** dē käts'ə
cow	**die Kuh** dē kōō
deer	**das Reh** däs rā
dog	**der Hund** dār hōōnt
eagle	**der Adler** dār äd'lər
fly	**die Fliege** dē flē'gə
fox	**der Fuchs** dār fōōks
frog	**der Frosch** dār frôsh
goat	**die Ziege** dē tsē'gə

hare	**der Hase** dār hä'zə
horse	**das Pferd** däs pfärt
lizard	**die Eidechse** dē ī'deksə
mosquito	**die Mücke** dē mįk'ə
mouse	**die Maus** dē mous
owl	**die Eule** dē oi'lə
pheasant	**der Fasan** dār fäzän'
pig	**das Schwein** däs shvīn
rabbit	**das Kaninchen** däs känēn'shən
rat	**die Ratte** dē rät'ə
seagull	**die Möwe** dē mā̱'və
sheep	**das Schaf** däs shäf
snake	**die Schlange** dē shläng'ə
sparrow	**der Spatz** dār späts
spider	**die Spinne** dē shpin'ə
stag	**der Hirsch** dār hirsh
tit	**die Meise** dē mī'zə
vulture	**der Geier** dār gī'ər
wasp	**die Wespe** dē ves'pə
wild boar	**das Wildschwein** däs vilt'shvīn

Plants

beech	**die Buche** dē bōō'hə
birch	**die Birke** dē bir'kə
broom	**der Ginster** dār gins'tər

5

chestnut	**der Kastanienbaum** dār kästä'nē·ənboum
heather	**die Heide** dē hi'də
larch	**die Lärche** dē ler'<u>sh</u>ə
maple	**der Ahorn** dār ä'hôrn
oak	**die Eiche** dē i'<u>sh</u>ə
pine	**die Kiefer** dē kē'fər
poplar	**die Pappel** dē päp'əl
spruce	**die Fichte** dē fi<u>sh</u>'tə
willow	**die Weide** dē vī'də

Shopping

BASIC PHRASES

Where can I get …? **Wo bekomme ich …?** vō bəkôm'ə ish …?

? Kann ich Ihnen helfen? May I help you?
• kän ish ē'nən hel'fən?

I'm just looking, **Danke, ich sehe mich nur um.**
thanks. däng'kə, ish sā'ə mish nōōr ōōm.

I'm being helped, **Danke, ich werde schon bedient.**
thanks. däng'kə, ish vār'də shōn bədēnt'.

I'd like … **Ich hätte gerne …** ish het'ə ger'nə …

a can of … **eine Dose …** i'nə dō'zə …
a bottle of … **eine Flasche …** i'nə fläsh'ə …
a jar of … **ein Glas …** īn gläs …
a package of … **eine Packung …** i'nə päk'ōōng …
a tube of … **eine Tube …** i'nə tōō'bə …

How much is/are …? **Was kostet/kosten …?** väs kôs'tət/kôs'tən …?

Could you show me **Können Sie mir noch etwas anderes**
something else? **zeigen?** ken'ən zē mēr nôh et'väs än'dərəs tsī'gən?

138

I'd like something less expensive.	**Ich hätte gern etwas Billigeres.** ish het'ə gern et'väs bil'igərəs.
I like this. I'll take it.	**Das gefällt mir. Ich nehme es.** däs gəfelt' mēr. ish nā'mə es.

6

? **Darf es sonst noch etwas sein?** därf es zônst nôh et'väs zin?	Will there be anything else?

That's all, thank you.	**Danke, das ist alles.** däng'kə, däs ist äl'əs.
Can I pay with this credit card?	**Kann ich mit dieser Kreditkarte zahlen?** kän ish mit dē'zər krädēt'kärtə tsä'lən?
Could you wrap it for traveling/giftwrap it, please?	**Können Sie es mir für die Reise/als Geschenk einpacken?** ken'ən zē es mēr fēr dē rī'zə/äls gəshengk' in'päkən?
Can you ship this to America for me?	**Können Sie mir das nach Amerika schicken?** ken'ən zē mēr däs näh ämā'rikä shik'ən?
Could I have a receipt, please?	**Kann ich bitte eine Quittung haben?** kän ish bit'ə i'nə kvit'ōōng hä'bən?
I'd like to exchange/return this.	**Ich möchte das umtauschen/zurückgeben.** ish mesh'tə däs ōōm'toushən/tsōōrık'gäbən.

139

Gehen Sie bitte zur Kunden-dienstabteilung. gā'ən zē bit'ə tsoor koon'dəndēnstäpti'loong.

You need to go to our customer-service department, please.

I'd like a refund, please.

Ich möchte mein Geld zurück. ish mesh'tə mīn gelt tsoorik'.

I think you've given me too little change back.

Ich glaube, Sie haben mir zu wenig herausgegeben. ish glou'bə, zē hä'bən mēr tsoo vā'nish herous'gəgē'bən.

INFO In large cities city center stores are usually open from 9 pm through to 8.30 pm. On Saturdays these stores are only open until 4 pm.

In suburban areas or in small towns stores usually close at 6 pm. Some of them even have a two-hour, or longer, break at midday. On a Saturday you might even find yourself standing in front of a locked door at 12 o'clock midday.

Hairdressing salons aren't usually open on Mondays.

General Vocabulary

bag	**die Tüte** dē tē̲'tə
better	**besser** bes'ər
(too) big	**(zu) groß** (tsoo) grōs
bigger	**größer** grā̲'sər
to buy	**kaufen** kou'fən

can	**die Dose** dē dōˈzə
cheaper	**billiger** bilˈigər
check	**der Scheck** dār shek
(too) conventional	**(zu) konventionell** (tsōō) kônventsyōnelˈ
(too) dark	**(zu) dunkel** (tsōō) dōōngˈkəl
to exchange	**umtauschen** ōōmˈtoushən
(too) expensive	**(zu) teuer** (tsōō) toiˈər
gift	**das Geschenk** däs gəshengkˈ
(too) hard	**(zu) hart** (tsōō) härt
(too) heavy	**(zu) schwer** (tsōō) shvār
jar	**das Glas** däs gläs
(too) light *(color)*	**(zu) hell** (tsōō) hel
(too) light *(weight)*	**(zu) leicht** (tsōō) līsht
(too) modern	**(zu) modern** (tsōō) mōdernˈ
to pack	**einpacken** īnˈpakən
present	**das Geschenk** däs gəshengkˈ
sale(s)	**der Ausverkauf** dār ousˈfərkouf
self-service	**die Selbstbedienung** dē selpstˈbədēnōōng
to serve	**bedienen** bədēˈnən
shop window	**das Schaufenster** däs shouˈfenstər
to show	**zeigen** tsīˈgən
(too) small	**(zu) klein** (tsōō) klīn
smaller	**kleiner** klīnər
(too) soft	**(zu) weich** (tsōō) vīsh

| special offer | **das Sonderangebot** däs zôn'dərän`gəbōt |
| square | **viereckig** vēr'ekish |

Colors and Patterns

beige	**beige** bāsh
black	**schwarz** shvärts
blue	**blau** blou
brown	**braun** broun
burgundy	**weinrot** vīn'rōt
checked	**kariert** kärērt'
colorful	**bunt** bōônt
cream-colored	**cremefarben** krām'färbən
dark	**dunkel** dōōng'kəl
dark blue	**dunkelblau** dōōng'kəlblou
gold(-colored)	**golden** gôl'dən
gray	**grau** grou
green	**grün** grēn
herringbone	**Fischgrät** fish'grāt
light	**hell** hel
patterned	**gemustert** gəmōōs'tərt
pink	**rosa** rō'zä
pinstripe	**Nadelstreifen** nä'dəlshtrīfən
purple	**lila** lē'lä
red	**rot** rōt
silver(y)	**silbern** zil'bərn

solid-color	**einfarbig** īn'färbi<u>sh</u>
striped	**gestreift** gəshtrīft'
turquoise	**türkis** tirkēs'
white	**weiß** vīs
yellow	**gelb** gelp

Materials

cotton	**die Baumwolle** dē boum'vôlə
lambswool	**die Lammwolle** dē läm'vôlə
loden	**der Loden** där lō'dən
natural fiber	**die Naturfaser** dē nätōōr'fäzər
pure new wool	**reine Schurwolle** rī'nə shōōr'vôlə
silk	**die Seide** dē zī'də
synthetic fiber	**die Synthetik** dē zintä'tik
wool	**die Wolle** dē vôl'ə

Stores

antique store	**das Antiquitätengeschäft** däs äntikvētä'təngəsheft'
barber	**der Friseur** där frizār'
bookstore	**die Buchhandlung** dē bōō<u>h</u>'händlōōng
candy store	**der Süßwarenladen** där zēs'värənlä'dən
department store	**das Kaufhaus** däs kouf'hous
drugstore	**die Drogerie** dē drōgərē'

dry cleaner's	**die Reinigung** dē rī'nigōōng
florist's	**das Blumengeschäft** däs blōō'məngəsheft'
hairdresser's	**der Friseur** dār frizār'
jeweler's	**der Juwelier** dār yōōvəlēr'
leather store	**das Lederwarengeschäft** däs lā'dərvärəngəsheft'
music store	**das Schallplattengeschäft** däs shäl'plätəngəsheft'
news(paper) store	**der Zeitungshändler** dār tsī'tōōngs·hend'lər
optician's	**der Optiker** dār ôp'tikər
perfume store	**die Parfümerie** dē pärfēmərē'
pharmacy	**die Apotheke** dē äpōtā'kə
photo shop	**das Fotogeschäft** däs fō'tōgəsheft
shoe repair shop	**der Schuhmacher** dār shōō'mähər
shoe store	**das Schuhgeschäft** däs shōō'gəsheft
souvenir store	**der Andenkenladen** dār än'dengkən·lä'dən
sporting goods store	**das Sportgeschäft** däs shpôrt'gəsheft
supermarket	**der Supermarkt** dār sōō'pərmärkt
tobacconist's	**der Tabakwarenladen** dār tä'bäkvärənlä'dən; *(Austria)* **die Trafik** dē träfēk'
watch repair shop	**der Uhrmacher** dār ōōr'mähər

144

INFO Americans will find this custom rather unusual: if you have been served personally by a shop assistant in a small store it is customary to say „Auf Wiedersehen" when leaving. In supermarkets and in larger stores you do so after you have paid at the cash register.

6

FOOD

What's that?	**Was ist das?** väs ist däs?	
Could I have ..., please?	**Kann ich bitte ...haben?** kän i<u>sh</u> bit'ə ... hä'bən?	
a pound of ...	**1 Pfund ...** in pfōōnt ...	
a serving of ...	**1 Portion ...** i'nə pôrtsyōn' ...	
a slice of ...	**1 Scheibe ...** i'nə shī'bə ...	
a piece of ...	**1 Stück ...** in shtĭk ...	
A little less, please.	**Etwas weniger, bitte.** et'väs vā'nigər, bit'ə.	
A little more, please.	**Etwas mehr, bitte.** et'väs mār, bit'ə.	
May I try some of that, please?	**Kann ich davon etwas probieren?** kän i<u>sh</u> dä'fôn et'väs prōbē'rən?	

145

Food

apple	**der Apfel** dār äp'fəl
apple juice	**der Apfelsaft** dār äp'fəlzäft
apricot	**die Aprikose** dē äprikō'zə
baby food	**die Babynahrung** dē bā'bēnä'rōōng
banana	**die Banane** dē bänä'nə
beans	**die Bohnen** *(plural)* dē bō'nən
beef	**das Rindfleisch** däs rint'flīsh
beer	**das Bier** däs bēr
boiled ham	**der gekochte Schinken** dār gəkōh'tə shing'kən
bread	**das Brot** däs brōt
butter	**die Butter** dē bōōt'ər
buttermilk	**die Buttermilch** dē bōōt'ərmilsh
cabbage	**der Kohl** dār kōl
cake	**der Kuchen** dār kōō'hən
canned goods	**die Konserven** *(plural)* dē kônzer'vən
carrots	**die Möhren** *(plural)* dē mȫ'rən
cheese	**der Käse** dār kā'zə
cherries	**die Kirschen** *(plural)* dē kir'shən
chicken	**das Hähnchen** däs hān'shən
chicory	**der Chicoree** dār shik'ōrā
chili peppers	**die Peperoni** *(plural)* dē peperō'nē
chives	**der Schnittlauch** dār shnit'louh
chocolate	**die Schokolade** dē shōkōlä'də

chocolates	**die Pralinen** *(plural)* dē prälē'nən
chop	**das Kotelett** däs kötlet'
cocoa	**der Kakao** där kä̱kou'
coffee	**der Kaffee** där kä̱f'ä
cold cuts	**der Aufschnitt** där ouf'shnit
cookies	**die Kekse** *(plural)* dē kāk'sə
corn	**der Mais** där mīs
cottage cheese	**der Quark** där kvärk
cream	**die Sahne** dē zä'nə
cucumber	**die Gurke** dē ḡoor'kə
cutlet	**das Schnitzel** däs shnit'səl
egg	**das Ei** däs ī
fish	**der Fisch** där fish
fruit	**das Obst** däs ōpst
garlic	**der Knoblauch** där knōp'louh
grapes	**die Weintrauben** *(plural)* dē vīn'troubən
green beans	**die grünen Bohnen** *(plural)* dē grē̱'nən bō'nən
ham	**der Schinken** där shing'kən
hamburger meat	**das Hackfleisch** däs häk'flīsh
honey	**der Honig** där hō'nish
ice cream	**das Eis** däs īs
iceberg lettuce	**der Eissalat** där īs'älät'
jam	**die Marmelade** dē mär'məlä'də
juice	**der Saft** där zäft

kiwi fruit	**die Kiwi** dē kē've
lamb	**das Lammfleisch** däs läm'flĭsh
leeks	**der Lauch** där lou<u>h</u>
lemon	**die Zitrone** dē tsĭt<u>r</u>ō'ne
lettuce	**der Salat** där zälät'
lima beans	**die weißen Bohnen** (plural) dē vī'sen bō'nen
lowfat milk	**die fettarme Milch** dē fet'ärme mĭl<u>sh</u>
macaroni	**die Makkaroni** (plural) dē mäkärō'nē
margarine	**die Margarine** dē märgerē'ne
mayonnaise	**die Mayonnaise** dē mäyōnä'ze
meat	**das Fleisch** däs flīsh
melon	**die Melone** dē melō'ne
milk	**die Milch** dē mĭl<u>sh</u>
non-alcoholic beer	**das alkoholfreie Bier** däs äl'kōhōlfrī·e bēr
nuts	**die Nüsse** (plural) dē nĭs'e
oil	**das Öl** däs äl
onion	**die Zwiebel** dē tsvē'bel
orange	**die Orange** dē ôräN'zhe
orange juice	**der Orangensaft** där ôräN'zhenzäft
paprika	**die Paprika** dē päp'rikä
parsley	**die Petersilie** dē päterzē'lē·e
pasta	**die Nudeln** (plural) dē nōō'deln
peach	**der Pfirsich** där pfir'si<u>sh</u>
peanuts	**die Erdnüsse** (plural) dē ärt'nĭse

148

pear	**die Birne** dē bir'nə
peas	**die Erbsen** *(plural)* dē er'psən
pepper *(spice)*	**der Pfeffer** dār pfef'ər
pepper *(vegetable)*	**die Paprikaschote** dē päp'rēkäshō'tə
pickles	**die eingelegten Gurken** dē īn'gəlägtən goor'kən
pineapple	**die Ananas** dē än'änäs
plums	**die Pflaumen** *(plural)* dē pflou'mən
pork	**das Schweinefleisch** däs shvī'nəflīsh
potatoes	**die Kartoffeln** *(plural)* dē kärtôf'əln
poultry	**das Geflügel** däs gəflē'gəl
raspberries	**die Himbeeren** *(plural)* dē him'bārən
red wine	**der Rotwein** dār rōt'vīn
rice	**der Reis** dār rīs
roll	**das Brötchen** däs brāt'shən
salad	**der Salat** dār zä'lät
salt	**das Salz** däs zälts
sandwich meats	**der Wurstaufschnitt** dār voorst'ouf'shnit
sausages	**die Würstchen** *(plural)* dē virst'shən
smoked ham	**der rohe Schinken** dār rō'ə shing'kən
soft drink	**die Limonade** dē lēmōnä'də
spices	**die Gewürze** *(plural)* dē gəvir'tsə
spinach	**der Spinat** dār shpēnät'
strawberries	**die Erdbeeren** *(plural)* dē ārt'bārən
sugar	**der Zucker** dār tsŏŏk'ər

6

sweetener	**der Süßstoff** dār zēs'shtôf
tea	**der Tee** dār tā
teabag	**der Teebeutel** dār tā'boitəl
tomato	**die Tomate** dē tōmä'tə
tuna	**der Thunfisch** dār tōōn'fish
veal	**das Kalbfleisch** däs kälp'flīsh
vegetables	**das Gemüse** däs gəmē'zə
vinegar	**der Essig** dār es'i<u>sh</u>
white wine	**der Weißwein** dār vīs'vīn
wine	**der Wein** dār vīn
yogurt	**der Jog(h)urt** dār yō'gōōrt

SOUVENIRS

What's typical of this area?	**Was gibt es Typisches von dieser Gegend?** väs gēbt es tē̲'pishəs fôn dē'zər gā'gənt?
Is this handmade?	**Ist das Handarbeit?** ist däs hänt'ärbīt?
Is this *antique/genuine*?	**Ist das *antik/echt*?** ist däs äntēk'/e<u>sh</u>t?

150

ceramics	**die Keramik** dē kerä'mik
certificate	**das Zertifikat** däs tser'tēfēkät'
china	**das Porzellan** däs pôrtsəlän'
earthenware	**das Steingut** däs stin'gōōt
hand-carved	**handgeschnitzt** hänt'gəshnitst
hand-knitted	**handgestrickt** hänt'gəshtrikt
handicraft(s)	**die Handarbeit** dē hänt'ärbīt
handmade	**handgemacht** hänt'gəmäht
handpainted	**handgemalt** hänt'gəmält
handwoven	**handgeknüpft** hänt'gəknipft
jewelry	**der Schmuck** dār shmōōk
jug	**die Kanne** dē kän'ə
leather	**das Leder** däs lā'dər
pottery	**die Keramik** dē kərä'mik
silver	**das Silber** däs zil'bər
souvenir	**das Andenken** däs än'dengkən
sweater	**der Pullover** dār pōōlō'vər
typical	**typisch** tē'pish

CLOTHES AND DRY CLEANER'S

I'm looking for …   **Ich suche …** i<u>sh</u> zōō'hə …

? **Welche Größe haben Sie?**   What size are you?
● vel'<u>sh</u>ə grā'sə hä'bən zē?

I'm a size …	**Ich habe Größe …** <u>ish</u> hä'bə grā'sə …
Do you have this in another *size/color*?	**Haben Sie das noch in einer anderen *Größe/Farbe*?** hä'bən zē däs nôh in ī'nər än'dərən grā'sə/fär'bə?

➡ *word list Colors and Patterns (p. 142)*

It's too *pale/dark*.	**Es ist zu *blass/dunkel*.** es ist tsōō bläs/dōōng'kəl.
May I try this on?	**Kann ich das anprobieren?** kän i<u>sh</u> däs än'prōbē'rən?
Do you have a mirror?	**Haben Sie einen Spiegel?** hä'bən zē ī'nən shpē'gəl?
Where are the fitting rooms?	**Wo sind die Umkleidekabinen?** vō zint dē ōōm'klīdəkäbē'nən?
What kind of material is this?	**Welches Material ist das?** vel'<u>sh</u>əs mäterē·äl' ist däs?
This is too *big/small*.	**Das ist mir zu *groß/klein*.** däs ist mēr tsōō grōs/klīn.
This fits nicely.	**Das passt gut.** däs päst gōōt.
I'd like this dry-cleaned.	**Ich möchte das reinigen lassen.** i<u>sh</u> me<u>sh</u>'tə däs rī'nigən läs'ən.

Clothes and Dry Cleaner's

6

anorak	**der Anorak** där än'örak
bathrobe	**der Bademantel** där bä'dəmäntəl
belt	**der Gürtel** där gir'təl
blouse	**die Bluse** dē blŏŏ'ze
bra	**der BH** där bähä'
button	**der Knopf** där knôpf
cap	**die Mütze** dē mit'sə
cardigan	**die Strickjacke** dē shtrik'yäkə
coat	**der Mantel** där män'təl
collar	**der Kragen** där krä'gən
color	**die Farbe** dē fär'bə
dirndl	**das Dirndl** däs dirn'dl
dress	**das Kleid** däs klīt
dressing gown	**der Morgenrock** där môr'gənrök
to dry-clean	**reinigen** rī'nigən
elegant	**elegant** ālāgänt'
gloves	**die Handschuhe** (plural) dē hänt'shŏŏ·ə
hat	**der Hut** där hŏŏt
hood	**die Kapuze** dē käpŏŏ'tsə
jacket	**die Jacke** dē yäk'ə
Janker jacket	**der Janker** där yäng'kər
lined	**gefüttert** gəfit'ərt
linen	**das Leinen** däs lī'nən

153

loden coat	**der Lodenmantel** dār lō'dənmän'təl
long	**lang** läng
man-made fiber	**die Synthetik** dē zintä'tik
nightgown	**das Nachthemd** däs näht'hemt
nightshirt	**das Nachthemd** däs näht'hemt
non-iron	**bügelfrei** bē'gəlfrī
pajamas	**der Schlafanzug** dār shläf'äntsook
panties	**der Slip** dār slip
pants	**die Hose** dē hō'zə
panty hose	**die Strumpfhose** dē shtroompf'hōzə
raincoat	**der Regenmantel** dār rā'gənmäntəl
scarf (*long*)	**der Schal** dār shäl
scarf (*square*)	**das Halstuch** däs häls'tōōh
shirt	**das Hemd** däs hemt
short	**kurz** koorts
shorts	**die Shorts** (*plural*) dē shôrts
size	**die Größe** dē grœ'sə
skirt	**der Rock** dār rôk
sleeve	**der Ärmel** dār är'məl
snap	**der Druckknopf** dār drook'nôpf
socks	**die Socken** (*plural*) dē zôk'ən
sports coat	**der Sakko** dār zäk'ō
stockings	**die Strümpfe** (*plural*) dē shtrim'pfə
suit	**der Anzug** dār än'tsook
suit	**das Kostüm** däs kôstēm'
sweater	**der Pullover** dār poolō'vər

sweatpants	**die Jogginghose** dē jôg'inghōzə
sweatsuit	**der Jogginganzug** dār jôg'ing·än'tsōōk
tie	**die Krawatte** dē krävät'ə
to try on	**anprobieren** än'prōbērən
underpants	**die Unterhose** dē ōōn'tərhōzə
undershirt	**das Unterhemd** däs ōōn'tərhemt
unusual	**ausgefallen** ous'gəfälən
to waterproof	**imprägnieren** impregnē'rən
zipper	**der Reißverschluss** dār ris'fərshlōōs

SHOES

I'd like a pair of …	**Ich möchte ein Paar …** ish mesh'tə īn pär …
My size is …	**Ich habe Schuhgröße …** ish hä'bə shōō'grṣə …
The heel is too *high/low* for me.	**Der Absatz ist mir zu *hoch/niedrig*.** dār äp'säts ist mēr tsōō *hōh/nē'drish*.
They're too tight around here.	**Sie drücken hier.** zē drik'ən hēr.

boots	**die Stiefel** *(plural)* dē shtē'fəl
crosstraining shoes	**die Turnschuhe** *(plural)* dē tōōrn'shōō·ə
heel	**der Absatz** dār äp'säts
hiking boots	**die Wanderschuhe** *(plural)* dē vän'dərshōō·ə
leather	**das Leder** däs lā'dər
mountain boots	**die Bergschuhe** *(plural)* dē berk'shōō·ə
open-toed shoes	**die offenen Schuhe** *(plural)* dē ôf'ənən shōō'ə
pumps	**die Pumps** *(plural)* dē pemps
rubber boots	**die Gummistiefel** *(plural)* dē gōōm'ēshtēfel
sandals	**die Sandalen** *(plural)* dē zändä'lən
shoe polish	**die Schuhcreme** dē shōō'krām
shoelaces	**die Schnürsenkel** *(plural)* dē shnēr'zengkel
shoes	**die Schuhe** *(plural)* dē shōō'ə
suede	**das Wildleder** däs vilt'lādər
tight	**eng** eng

WATCHES AND JEWELRY

My watch is *fast/slow.*	**Meine Uhr geht *vor/nach.*** mī'nə ōōr gāt fôr/näḫ.
What's this made of?	**Woraus ist das?** vōrous' ist däs?
What percentage silver does it have?	**Wie hoch ist der Silberanteil?** vē hōḫ ist der zil'bərän'tīl?
How many carats is it?	**Wie hoch ist der Goldanteil?** vē hōḫ ist dār gôlt'än'tīl?

Watches and Jewelry

battery	**die Batterie** dē bätərē'
bracelet	**das Armband** däs ärm'bänt
brooch	**die Brosche** dē brôsh'ə
carat	**das Karat** däs kärät'
clip-on earrings	**die Ohrklipse** *(plural)* dē ōr'klipsə
costume jewelry	**der Modeschmuck** dēr mō'dəshmōōk
diamonds	**die Brillanten** *(plural)***, die Diamanten** *(plural)* dē bril'yäntən, dē dē·ämän'tən
earrings	**die Ohrringe** *(plural)* dē ôr'ingə
gold	**das Gold** däs gôlt
gold-plated	**vergoldet** fərgôl'dət
necklace	**die Halskette** dē häls'ketə
pearl	**die Perle** dē per'lə

pendant	**der Anhänger** dēr än'hengər
platinum	**das Platin** däs plä'tēn
ring	**der Ring** dār ring
ruby	**der Rubin** dār rōōbēn'
silver	**das Silber** däs zil'bər
silver-plated	**versilbert** fərzil'bərt
watch	**die Uhr** dē ōōr
watchband	**das Uhrenarmband** däs ōōr'ənärm`bänt

PERSONAL HYGIENE AND HOUSEHOLD

Personal Hygiene

aftershave	**das Aftershave** däs äf'tərshāv
baby bottle	**die Babyflasche** dē bā'bēfläshə
baby bottle nipple	**der Sauger** dār zou'gər
baby oil	**das Babyöl** däs bā'bē·āl'
baby powder	**der Babypuder** dār bā'bēpōō'dər
barrette	**die Haarspange** dē här'shpängə
brush	**die Bürste** dē birs'tə
cleansing cream	**die Reinigungsmilch** dē rī'nigōōngsmil<u>sh</u>
comb	**der Kamm** dār käm
condom	**das Kondom** däs kôndōm'
cotton	**die Watte** dē vät'ə
cotton swabs	**die Wattestäbchen** *(plural)* dē vät'əsht<u>ä</u>b<u>sh</u>ən

158

curlers	**die Lockenwickler** *(plural)* dē lôk'ənviklər
dandruff shampoo	**das Shampoo gegen Schuppen** däs shäm'pōō gā'gən shōōp'ən
day cream	**die Tagescreme** dē tä'gəskrām
dental floss	**die Zahnseide** dē tsän'zīdə
deodorant	**das Deo** däs dā'ō
depilatory cream	**die Enthaarungscreme** dē ent·hä'rōōngskrām
detergent	**das Waschmittel** däs väsh'mitəl
diapers	**die Windeln** *(plural)* dē vin'dəln
disposable towels	**die Einweghandtücher** *(plural)* dē īn'vāk·hän'tēshər
disposable wipes	**die Einwegwaschlappen** *(plural)* dē īn'vāk·väsh'läpən
elastic hairband	**das Haargummi** däs här'gōōmē
eye shadow	**der Lidschatten** dār lēt'shätən
fragrance-free	**parfümfrei** pärfēm'frī
hair dryer	**der Haartrockner** dār här'trôknər
hairclips	**die Haarklammern** *(plural)* dē här'klämərn
hairspray	**der Haarspray** dār här'shprā
handcream	**die Handcreme** dē hänt'krām
handkerchiefs	**die Taschentücher** *(plural)* dē täsh'əntēshər

lip balm	**der Lippenpflegestift** där lip'ənpflä`gəshtift
lipstick	**der Lippenstift** där lip'ənshtift
makeup remover	**der Make-up-Entferner** där mäk'äp-entfer`nər
mascara	**die Wimperntusche** dē vim'pərntōōshə
mosquito repellent	**der Mückenschutz** där mik'ənshōōts
mousse	**der Schaumfestiger** där shoum'festigər
nailbrush	**die Nagelbürste** dē nä'gəlbirstə
nail file	**die Nagelfeile** dē nä'gəlfīlə
nail polish	**der Nagellack** där nä'gəläk
nail polish remover	**der Nagellackentferner** där nä'gəläkentfer`nər
nail scissors	**die Nagelschere** dē nä'gəlshārə
night cream	**die Nachtcreme** dē näht'krām
pacifier	**der Schnuller** där shnōōl'ər
perfume	**das Parfüm** däs pärfēm'
pH balanced	**ph-neutral** pähä'-noiträl
plaster	**das Pflaster** däs pfläs'tər
powder	**der Puder** där pōō'dər
razor blade	**die Rasierklinge** dē räzēr'klingə
sanitary napkins	**die Damenbinden** *(plural)* dē dä'mənbindən
shampoo	**das Shampoo** däs shäm'pōō
shampoo for normal hair	**das Shampoo für normales Haar** däs shäm'pōō fēr nôrmä'ləs här

shampoo for oily hair	**das Shampoo für fettiges Haar** däs shäm'pōō fer fet'iges här
shaver	**der Rasierapparat** där räzēr'äpärät'
shaving cream	**die Rasiercreme** dē räzēr'krām
shaving foam	**der Rasierschaum** där räzēr'shoum
skin cream	**die Hautcreme** dē hout'krām
– for dry skin	**für trockene Haut** fer trôk'ənə hout
– for normal skin	**für normale Haut** fer nôrmä'lə hout
– for oily skin	**für fettige Haut** fer fet'ige hout
soap	**die Seife** dē zi'fə
stain remover	**der Fleckentferner** där flek'entfer'nər
styling gel	**das Haargel** däs här'gäl
sun protection factor	**der Lichtschutzfaktor** där lisht'shōōtsfäk'tôr
suntan oil	**das Sonnenöl** däs zôn'ənäl
talcum powder	**der Körperpuder** där ker'pərpōōdər
tampons	**die Tampons** *(plural)* dē täm'pôns
tissues	**die Papiertaschentücher** *(plural)* dē päpēr'täshəntē'shər
toilet tissue	**das Toilettenpapier** däs tô·älet'ənpäpēr
toothbrush	**die Zahnbürste** dē tsän'bırstə
toothpaste	**die Zahnpasta** dē tsän'pästä
toothpick	**der Zahnstocher** där tsän'shtôhər
tweezers	**die Pinzette** dē pintset'ə
washcloth	**der Waschlappen** där väsh'läpən

161

alarm clock	**der Wecker** dār vek'ər
aluminum foil	**die Alufolie** dē ä'lo͞ofo͞'lē·ə
bottle opener	**der Flaschenöffner** dār fläsh'ənęfnər
broom	**der Besen** dār bā'zən
can opener	**der Dosenöffner** dār dō'zənęfnər
candle	**die Kerze** dē ker'tsə
charcoal	**die Grillkohle** dē gril'kōlə
cleaning material	**das Reinigungsmittel** däs rī'nigo͞ongs-mit'əl
corkscrew	**der Korkenzieher** dār kôr'kəntsē·ər
cup	**die Tasse** dē täs'ə
denatured alcohol	**der Brennspiritus** dār bren'shpērito͞os
detergent	**das Waschmittel** däs väsh'mitəl
dish detergent	**das Spülmittel** däs shpēl'mitəl
extension cord	**die Verlängerungsschnur** dē fərleng'əro͞ongs-shno͞or
flashlight	**die Taschenlampe** dē täsh'ənlämpə
fork	**die Gabel** dē gä'bəl
gas cartridge	**die Gaskartusche** dē gäs'kärto͞osh·ə
glass	**das Glas** däs gläs
grill	**der Grill** dār gril
insect repellent	**der Insektenspray** dār insek'tənsprā
kitchen paper	**das Küchenpapier** däs kish'ənpäpēr
knife	**das Messer** däs mes'ər

light bulb	**die Glühlampe** dē glē'lämpə
lighter	**das Feuerzeug** däs foi'ərtsoik
matches	**die Streichhölzer** *(plural)* dē
	shtri<u>sh</u>'heltsər
napkins	**die Servietten** *(plural)* dē zervē·et'ən
pail	**der Eimer** dār i'mər
pan	**die Pfanne** dē pfän'ə
paper cup	**der Pappbecher** dār päp'beshər
paper plate	**der Pappteller** dār päp'telər
plastic wrap	**die Frischhaltefolie** dē
	frish'hältəfō'lē·e
plate	**der Teller** dār tel'ər
pocket knife	**das Taschenmesser** däs täsh'ənmesər
pot	**der Topf** dār tôpf
safety pin	**die Sicherheitsnadel** dē
	zi<u>sh</u>'ərhītsnä'dəl
scissors	**die Schere** dē shā're
sewing needle	**die Nähnadel** dē nā'nädəl
sewing thread	**das Nähgarn** däs nā'gärn
spoon	**der Löffel** dār le̦'fəl
string	**der Bindfaden** dār bint'fädən
thermos bottle®	**die Thermosflasche®** dē ter'môsfläshə

6

AT THE OPTICIAN'S

My glasses are broken.	**Meine Brille ist kaputt.** mī'nə bril'ə ist käpōōt'.
Can you fix this?	**Können Sie das reparieren?** ken'ən zē däs repärē'rən?
I'm *nearsighted/farsighted*.	**Ich bin *kurzsichtig/weitsichtig*.** ish bin kōōrts'zishtish/vīt'zishtish.
I'd like a pair of sunglasses.	**Ich möchte eine Sonnenbrille.** ish mesh'tə ī'nə zôn'ənbrilə.
I've *lost/broken* a contact lens.	**Ich habe eine Kontaktlinse *verloren/kaputtgemacht*.** ish hä'bə ī'nə kôntäkt'linzə ferlō'rən/käpōōt'gəmäht.
I need some *rinsing/cleaning* solution for *hard/soft* contact lenses.	**Ich brauche *Aufbewahrungslösung/Reinigungslösung* für *harte/weiche* Kontaktlinsen.** ish brou'hə ouf'bəvärōōngslā'zōōng/rī'nigōōngs-lā'zōōng fēr här'tə/vī'she kôntäkt'linzen.

AT THE HAIRDRESSER'S

I'd like to make an appointment for …	**Ich hätte gern einen Termin für …** ish het'ə gern ī'nən termēn' fēr …

? Was wird bei Ihnen gemacht? What would you like
• väs virt bī ē'nən gəm<u>ä</u>ht'?   to have done?

I'd like …   **Ich möchte …** i<u>sh</u> me<u>sh</u>'tə …

to have my hair cut. **mir die Haare schneiden lassen.**
          mēr dē hä'rə shnī'dən l<u>ä</u>s'ən.

a perm.   **eine Dauerwelle.** ī'nə dou'ərvelə.

some highlights put in. **Strähnchen.** shtr<u>ä</u>n'<u>sh</u>ən.

my hair tinted.   **eine Tönung.** ī'nə t<u>ä</u>'nōōng.

Just a cut, please. **Bitte nur schneiden.** bit'ə nōōr
          shnī'dən.

Cut, wash and   **Schneiden, waschen und föhnen, bitte.**
blow-dry, please.   shnī'dən, v<u>ä</u>sh'ən ōōnt f<u>ä</u>'nən, bit'ə.

? Wie hätten Sie's denn gern? How would you like
• vē het'ən zēs den gern?   it?

Not too short, please. **Nicht zu kurz, bitte.** ni<u>sh</u>t tsōō
          kōōrts, bit'ə.

A little shorter/Very ***Etwas kürzer/Ganz kurz, bitte.***
short, please.   et'v<u>ä</u>s k<u>i</u>r'tsər/g<u>ä</u>nts kōōrts, bit'ə.

Part it on the *left/right,* **Den Scheitel bitte *links/rechts.***
please.   dän shī'təl bit'ə *lingks/re<u>sh</u>ts.*

That looks good,   **Vielen Dank, das sieht gut aus.**
thank you.   vē'lən d<u>ä</u>ngk, d<u>ä</u>s zēt gōōt ous.

At the Hairdresser's

bangs	**der Pony**	dār pô'nē
beard	**der Bart**	dār bärt
blond(e)	**blond**	blônt
to blow-dry	**föhnen**	fā'nən
dandruff	**die Schuppen** *(plural)*	dē shōōp'ən
to dye	**färben**	fār'bən
gel	**das Gel**	däs gāl
hair	**das Haar**	däs här
highlights	**die Strähnchen** *(plural)*	dē shtrān'shən
layered cut	**der Stufenschnitt**	dār shtōō'fənshnit
perm	**die Dauerwelle**	dē dou'ərvelə
razor cut	**der Messerschnitt**	dār mes'ərshnit
tint	**die Tönung**	dē tā'nōōng
to wash	**waschen**	väsh'ən

PHOTO AND VIDEO

I'd like …	**Ich hätte gern …**	i<u>sh</u> het'ə gern …
some film for this camera.	**einen Film für diesen Apparat.**	ī'nən film fēr dē'zən äpärät'.
a color print film.	**einen Farbnegativfilm.**	ī'nən färb'negätēf film.
a slide film.	**einen Diafilm.**	ī'nən dē'äfilm.

a 24/36 exposure film.	**einen Film mit 24/36 Aufnahmen.** ī'nən film mit fēr'ōōntsvän'tsisḥ/ zeks'ōōntrī'sisḥ ouf'nämən.
a VHS video cassette.	**eine VHS-Videokassette.** ī'nə fou´-hä-es' vē'dā-ōkäset'ə.
I'd like some batteries for this camera.	**Ich hätte gerne Batterien für diesen Apparat.** isḥ het'ə ger'nə bätərē'ən fēr dē'zən äpärät'.
Could you please put the film in for me?	**Können Sie mir bitte den Film ein-legen?** ken'ən zē mēr bit'ə dän film īn'lāgən?
I'd like to get this film processed.	**Ich möchte diesen Film entwickeln lassen.** isḥ mesḥ'tə dē'zən film ent-vik'əln läs'ən.
Can you repair my camera?	**Können Sie meinen Fotoapparat reparieren?** ken'ən zē mī'nən fō'tō·äpärät repärē'rən?
The film doesn't wind forward.	**Er transportiert nicht.** är tränspôrtērt' nisḥt.
The *shutter release/ flash* doesn't work.	***Der Auslöser/Das Blitzlicht* funktio-niert nicht.** dār ous'lāzər /däs blits'lisḥt fōōngktsyōnērt' nisḥt.

Photo and Video

camcorder	**die Videokamera** dē vē'dā-ōkä̲ mərä
camera	**der Fotoapparat** dār fō'tō-äpärät
color film	**der Farbfilm** dār färb'film
to expose	**belichten** bəli<u>sh</u>'tən
exposure meter	**der Belichtungsmesser** dār bəli<u>sh</u>'tōōngsmesər
to film	**filmen** fil'mən
flash	**der Blitz** dār blits
lens	**das Objektiv** däs ôpyektēv'
lens cap	**der Objektivdeckel** dār ôpyektēv'dekəl
negative	**das Negativ** däs nä'gätēv
personal stereo	**der Walkman** (Wz.) dār vôk'mən
photo	**das Bild** däs bilt
slide	**das Dia** däs dē'ä
slide film	**der Diafilm** dār dē'äfilm
SLR camera	**die Spiegelreflexkamera** dē shpē'gəlrefleks·käm`ärä
telephoto lens	**das Teleobjektiv** däs tā'lā·ôpyektēv
video camera	**die Videokamera** dē vē'dā·ōkä̲ mərä
video cassette	**die Videokassette** dē vē'dā·ōkäset'ə
Walkman®	**der Walkman**® dār vôk'mən
wide-angle lens	**das Weitwinkelobjektiv** däs vīt'vingkelôpyektēv'
zoom lens	**das Zoomobjektiv** däs zōōm'ôpyektēv'

READING AND WRITING

Do you have any American newspapers?	**Haben Sie amerikanische Zeitungen?** häˈbən zē ämärikäˈnishə tsiˈtoō͝ŋgən?
Do you have a more recent edition?	**Haben Sie eine neuere Zeitung?** häˈbən zē īˈnə noiˈərə tsiˈtoō͝ng?
Do you have stamps?	**Haben Sie auch Briefmarken?** häˈbən zē ou͟h brēfˈmärkən?

Reading and Writing

adhesive tape	**das Klebeband** däs klāˈbəbänt
ball point pen	**der Kugelschreiber** där koō͝gəlshrībər
city map	**der Stadtplan** där shtätˈplän
comic book	**das Comic-Heft** däs kômˈik-heft
cookbook	**das Kochbuch** däs kôh̲ˈboō͟h
dictionary	**das Wörterbuch** däs verˈtərboō͟h
envelope	**der Briefumschlag** där brēfˈoō͝omshläk
glue	**der Klebstoff** där klāpˈshtôf
hiking trail map	**die Wanderkarte** dē vänˈdərkärtə
paper	**das Papier** däs päpērˈ
pencil	**der Bleistift** där blīˈshtift
picture book	**das Bilderbuch** däs bilˈdərboō͟h
postcard	**die Ansichtskarte** dē änˈzishts·kärˈtə
road map	**die Straßenkarte** dē shträˈsənkärˈtə
stamp	**die Briefmarke** dē brēfˈmärkə

travel guide	**der Reiseführer** dār rī'zəfērər
wrapping paper	**das Geschenkpapier** dās gəshengk'päpēr
writing paper	**das Briefpapier** däs brēf'päpēr

AT THE TOBACCONIST'S

A pack of …, *filters/ non-filter*, please.
Eine Schachtel … *mit/ohne* Filter, bitte. ī'nə shäh'təl … *mit/ō'nə* fil'tər, bit'ə.

A pack/A carton of …, please.
Eine Schachtel/Eine Stange …, bitte. *ī'nə shäh'təl/ī'nə shtäng'ə …, bit'ə.*

A can of … pipe tobacco, please.
Eine Dose … Pfeifentabak, bitte. ī'nə dō'ze … pfī'fəntäbäk, bit'ə.

Could I have *some matches/a lighter*, please?
Könnte ich bitte *Streichhölzer/ein Feuerzeug* haben? ken'tə ish bit'ə *shtrīsh'heltsər/īn foi'ertsoik* hä'bən?

Entertainment and Sports

SWIMMING AND WATER SPORTS

At the Beach

How do *I/we* get to the beach? **Wo geht es zum Strand?**
vō gāt es tsōōm shtränt?

Is swimming permitted here? **Darf man hier baden?**
därf män hēr bä'dən?

How *deep/warm* is the water? **Wie tief/warm ist das Wasser?**
vē tēf/värm ist däs väs'ər?

How far out can one swim? **Wie weit darf man hinaus-schwimmen?** vē vit därf män
hinous'shvimən?

Bis ... bis ...   As far as ...

! **zur Boje.** tsōōr bō'ye.   the buoy.
zum Felsen. tsōōm fel'sən.   the rock.
zur Markierung. tsōōr   the marker.
märkē'rōōng.

Are there currents here? **Gibt es hier Strömungen?**
gēpt es hēr shtrā'mōōngən?

When is *low/high* tide? **Wann ist *Ebbe/Flut*?** vän ist
eb'ə/flōōt?

Is it dangerous for children?	**Ist es für Kinder gefährlich?**
	ist es für kin'dər gəfär'li<u>sh</u>?
Are there jellyfish around here?	**Gibt es hier Quallen?**
	gēpt es hēr kväl'ən?
Where can I rent …?	**Wo kann man … ausleihen?** vō kän
	män … ous'lī·ən?
I'd like to go waterskiing.	**Ich möchte Wasserski fahren.**
	i<u>sh</u> me<u>sh</u>'tə väs'ərshē fä'rən.
I'd like to take *diving/ windsurfing* lessons.	**Ich möchte einen *Tauchkurs/ Windsurfkurs* machen.** i<u>sh</u> me<u>sh</u>'tə
	ī'nən *tou<u>h</u>'kōōrs/vint'serfkōōrs* mä<u>h</u>'ən.
Would you mind keeping an eye on my things for a moment, please?	**Würden Sie bitte kurz auf meine Sachen aufpassen?** vir'dən sē bit'ə
	kōōrts ouf mī'nə zä<u>h</u>'ən ouf'päsən?

INFO On many beaches in the north of Germany you are required to pay a health resort tax before you are allowed to use them. If you also want to hire for the day one of the covered wicker beach chairs, which are so typical of the region, it will cost you and your family quite a lot, even before you have done as much as dip your toe in the water.

7

173

At the Swimming Pool

What coins do I need for the *lockers/hair-dryers*?	**Welche Münzen brauche ich für *das Schließfach/den Haartrockner*?**
	vel'shə min'tsən brou'hə ish fēr *däs shlēs'fäh/dān här'trôknər*?
I'd like to *rent/buy* ...	**Ich möchte ... *ausleihen/kaufen.*** ish mesh'tə ... *ous'lī-ən/kou'fən.*
a swimming cap.	**eine Badekappe** ī'nə bä'dəkäpə
a towel.	**ein Handtuch** īn hän'tōōh
some water wings.	**Schwimmflügel** shvim'flēgəl
Are there swimming lessons for *children/adults*?	**Gibt es Schwimmunterricht für *Kinder/Erwachsene*?** gēpt es shvim'ōōntərisht fēr *kin'dər/erväk'sənə*?
Where's the *lifeguard/first-aid station*?	**Wo ist *der Bademeister/die Sanitäts-stelle*?** vō ist *dār bä'dəmīstər/dē sänitäts'shtelə*?

INFO Some indoor swimming-pools require both males and females to wear swimming caps. If you don't have a cap you can hire one at the pay desk for a small charge.

air mattress	**die Luftmatratze** dē lōoft'mäträtsə
bathing cap	**die Badekappe** dē bä'dəkäpə
bathing suit	**der Badeanzug** dār bä'də·äntsōōk
bay	**die Bucht** dē bōōht
beach	**der Strand** dār shtränt
bikini	**der Bikini** dār bēkē'nē
boat	**das Boot** däs bōt
boat rental	**der Bootsverleih** dār bōts'fərlī
changing cubicle	**die Umkleidekabine** dē ōōm'klīdə·käbē'nə
current	**die Strömung** dē shtrā'mōōng
deckchair	**der Liegestuhl** dār lē'gəshtōōl
deep	**tief** tēf
depth of the water	**die Wassertiefe** dē väs'ərtēfə
to dive	**tauchen** tou'hən
diving board	**das Sprungbrett** däs shprōōng'bret
diving equipment	**die Taucherausrüstung** dē tou'hər·ous`ristōōng
diving mask	**die Tauchermaske** dē tou'hərmäskə
diving platform	**der Sprungturm** dār shprōōng'tōōrm
diving suit	**der Taucheranzug** dār tou'həräntsōōk
fins	**die Schwimmflossen** *(plural)* dē shvim'flôsən
high tide	**die Flut** dē flōōt

7

inflatable boat	**das Schlauchboot** däs shlouh'bōt
jellyfish	**die Qualle** dē kväl'ə
lifeguard	**der Bademeister** dār bä'dəmīstər
lifesaver	**der Rettungsring** dār ret'ōōngsring
low tide	**die Ebbe** dē eb'ə
motorboat	**das Motorboot** däs mō'tōrbōt
non-swimmer	**der Nichtschwimmer** dār nisht'shvimər
nude beach	**der FKK-Strand** dār ef-kä-kä'-shtränt
pool	**das Schwimmbad** däs shvim'bät
to row	**rudern** rōō'dərn
rowboat	**das Ruderboot** däs rōō'dərbōt
to sail	**segeln** zā'gəln
sailboat	**das Segelboot** däs zā'gəlbōt
sand	**der Sand** dār zänt
sandy beach	**der Sandstrand** dār zänt'shtränt
shade	**der Schatten** dār shät'ən
shells	**die Muscheln** *(plural)* dē mōōsh'əln
shower	**die Dusche** dē dōōsh'ə
snorkel	**der Schnorchel** dār shnôr'shəl
storm	**der Sturm** dār shtōōrm
storm tide	**die Sturmflut** dē shtōōrm'flōōt
storm warning	**die Sturmwarnung** dē shtōōrm'- värnōōng
to sunbathe	**sich sonnen** zish zôn'ən
sunglasses	**die Sonnenbrille** dē zôn'ənbrilə
suntan lotion	**die Sonnencreme** dē zôn'ənkrām

surfboard	**das Surfbrett** däs serf'bret
to swim	**schwimmen** shvim'ən
swim goggles	**die Schwimmbrille** dē shvim'brilə
swim trunks	**die Badehose** dē bä'dəhōzə
towel	**das Handtuch** däs hän'tōōh
water	**das Wasser** däs väs'ər
water polo	**das Wasserballspiel** däs väs'ərbälshpēl
water ski	**der Wasserski** där väs'ərshē
water temperature	**die Wassertemperatur** dē väs'ər-temperätōōr
water wings	**die Schwimmflügel** (plural) dē shvim'flēgəl
wave	**die Welle** dē vel'ə
wetsuit	**der Surfanzug** där serf'äntsōōk
to windsurf	**surfen** ser'fən

7

MOUNTAINEERING

I'd like to take a … -hour walk.

Ich möchte eine …stündige Wanderung machen. ish mesh'tə i'nə …shtin'digə vän'dərōōng mäh'ən.

I'd like to *go to/ climb* …

Ich möchte *nach/auf den* … ish mesh'tə *näh/ouf dän* …

Can you recommend *an easy/a moderately difficult* hiking trail?	**Können Sie mir eine *leichte/mittelschwere* Tour empfehlen?** kẹn'ən zē mēr i'nə *lịsh'tə/mit'əlshvārə* tōōr empfā'lən?
Approximately how long will it take?	**Wie lange dauert sie ungefähr?** vē lặng'ə dou'ərt zē ōōn'gəfār?
Is the path *well marked/secure*?	**Ist der Weg *gut markiert/gesichert*?** ist dār vāk *gōōt märkērt'/gəzịsh'ərt*?
Can I go in these shoes?	**Kann ich in diesen Schuhen gehen?** kặn ịsh in dē'zən shōō'ən gā'ən?
Is this the right way to …?	**Ist dies der richtige Weg nach …?** ist dēs dār rịsh'tigə vāk näh …?
How much farther is it to …?	**Wie weit ist es noch bis …?** vē vīt ist es nô̱h bis …?

INFO There is a large network of well-signposted trails in the Alps, each of which takes you to a mountain cabin after about three or four hours walking. Most of these cabins are run commercially. You can get something to eat there or spend the night. If you want a certain degree of comfort on your mountain hike you should book a night stay in advance or else you might find yourself sharing floorspace in a large room with around twenty others.

Mountaineering

cable car	**die Seilbahn** dē zīl'bän
to climb	**klettern** klet'ərn
climbing boots	**die Bergschuhe** *(plural)* dē berk'shōō·ə
crampon	**das Steigeisen** däs shtīk'īzən
to have a head for heights	**schwindelfrei sein** shvin'dəlfrī zīn
to hike	**wandern** vän'dərn
hike	**die Tour** dē tōōr
hiking map	**die Wanderkarte** dē vän'dərkärtə
hiking trail	**der Wanderweg** där vän'dərvāk
hut	**die Hütte** dē hit'ə
mountain	**der Berg** där berk
mountain climbing	**das Bergsteigen** däs berk'shtīgən
mountain guide	**der Bergführer** där berk'fērər
mountain rescue service	**die Bergwacht** dē berk'väht
provisions	**der Proviant** där prōvē·änt'
ravine	**die Schlucht** dē shlōōht
rope	**das Seil** däs zīl
trail	**der Weg** där vāk

7

MORE SPORTS AND GAMES

Do you have any
playing cards/board
games?

**Haben Sie _Spielkarten/Gesellschafts-
spiele_?** hä'bən zē _shpēl'kärtən/
gəzel'shäfts·shpē'lə_?

Do you play chess?

Spielen Sie Schach? shpē'lən zē shäḫ?

What kind of sporting
activities are there
here?

**Welche Sportmöglichkeiten gibt es
hier?** vel'shə shpôrt'mäglishkī'tən gēpt
es hēr?

Do you mind if I join
in?

Darf ich mitspielen?
därf ish mit'shpēlən?

We'd like to rent a
tennis court/squash
court for an hour/half
an hour.

**Wir hätten gern einen _Tennisplatz/
Squashcourt_ für _eine/eine halbe_
Stunde.** vēr het'ən gern ī'nən
ten'ispläts/skvôsh'kôrt fēr ī'nə/ī'nə
häl'bə shtoon'də.

Sports and Games

athletic	**sportlich** shpôrt'lish
athletics	**die Leichtathletik** dē lisht'ätlā'tik
badminton	**das Federballspiel** däs fā'dərbälshpēl
bait	**der Köder** dār kë'dər
ball	**der Ball** dār bäl
beginner	**der Anfänger** dār än'fengər

bicycle, bike	**das Fahrrad**	däs fä'rät
bicycle tour	**die Radtour**	dē rä'tōōr
to bike, to go biking	**Rad fahren**	rät fä'rən
to bowl, to go bowling	**kegeln**	kā'gəln
bowling alley	**die Kegelbahn**	dē kā'gəlbän
bungee-jumping	**das Bungee-Springen**	däs bän'jē-shpringən
canoe	**das Kanu**	däs kä'nōō
card game	**das Kartenspiel**	däs kär'tənshpēl
championship	**die Meisterschaft**	dē mīs'tərshäft
changing rooms	**die Umkleideräume** *(plural)*	dē ōōm'klīdəroimə
chess	**das Schach**	däs shäh
chessboard	**das Schachbrett**	däs shäh'bret
chessmen	**die Schachfiguren** *(plural)*	dē shäh'figōōrən
coach	**der Trainer**	dār trā'nər
coaching session	**die Trainerstunde**	dē trā'nərshtōōndə
competition	**der Wettkampf**	dār wet'kämpf
course	**der Kurs**	dār kōōrs
to cycle	**Rad fahren**	rät fä'rən
it was a draw	**es war unentschieden**	es vär ōōn'entshē'dən
fencing	**das Fechten**	däs fesh'tən
final score	**das Endergebnis**	däs end'ergäbnis

finishing line	**das Ziel** däs tsēl
to fish	**angeln** äng'əln
fishing hook	**der Angelhaken** dār äng'əlhäkən
fishing license	**der Angelschein** dār äng'əlshīn
fishing rod	**die Angel** dē äng'əl
game	**das Spiel** däs shpēl
goal	**das Tor** däs tōr
goalkeeper	**der Torwart** dār tōr'värt
golf	**das Golf** däs gôlf
golf club	**der Golfschläger** dār gôlf'shlägər
golf course	**der Golfplatz** dār gôlf'pläts
gymnastics	**die Gymnastik** dē gimnäs'tik
to do gymnastics	**turnen** tōōr'nən
half-time	**die Halbzeit** dē hälp'tsīt
handball	**der Handball** dār hänt'bäl
hang-gliding	**das Drachenfliegen** däs dräh'ənflēgən
hockey	**das Eishockey** däs īs'hôkē
horse	**das Pferd** däs pfärt
horse racing	**das Pferderennen** däs pfär'dərenən
kayak	**der Kajak** dār kä'yäk
match	**das Spiel** däs shpēl
mini-golf course	**der Minigolfplatz** dār min'ēgôlfpläts
parasailing	**das Gleitschirmfliegen** däs glīt'shirmflēgən
to play	**spielen** shpē'lən
playing cards	**die Spielkarten** *(plural)* dē shpēl'kärtən

program	**das Programm** däs prōgräm'
referee	**der Schiedsrichter** dār shēts'ri̱shtər
to ride	**reiten** rī'tən
to row	**rudern** rōō'dern
skydiving	**das Fallschirmspringen** däs fäl'-shirmshpring`ən
soccer	**der Fußball** dār fōōs'bäl
soccer field	**der Fußballplatz** dār fōōs'bälpläts
solarium	**das Solarium** däs sōlä'rē-ōōm
sport(s)	**der Sport** dār shpôrt
sports ground	**der Sportplatz** dār shpôrt'pläts
start	**der Start** dār shtärt
table tennis	**das Tischtennis** däs tish'tenis
table tennis ball	**der Tischtennisball** dār tish'tenisbäl
table tennis bat	**der Tischtennisschläger** dār tish'tenis·shlā`gər
team	**die Mannschaft** dē män'shäft
tennis	**das Tennis** däs ten'is
tennis ball	**der Tennisball** dār ten'isbäl
tennis court	**der Tennisplatz** dār ten'ispläts
tennis racket	**der Tennisschläger** dār ten'is·shlā`gər
water polo	**das Wasserballspiel** däs väs'ərbälshpēl
win	**der Sieg** dār zēk

7

CULTURE AND FESTIVALS

At the Box Office

ausverkauft ous'fərkouft	sold out
der Eingang dār īn'gäng	entrance
die Galerie dē gälərē'	gallery
links lingks	left
die Loge dē lō'zhə	box
die Mitte dē mit'ə	middle
der Notausgang dār nōt'ousgäng	emergency exit
das Parkett däs pärket'	orchestra
der Platz dār pläts	seat
der Rang dār räng	balcony
rechts reshts	right
die Reihe dē rī'ə	row

What's on tonight? — **Was wird heute Abend gespielt?** väs virt hoi'tə ä'bənt gəshpēlt'?

When does the *performance/concert* start? — **Wann beginnt *die Vorstellung/das Konzert*?** vän bəgint' *dē fōrshtelōōng/däs kôntsert'*?

Are the seats numbered? — **Sind die Plätze nummeriert?** zint dē plet'sə nōōmərērt'?

184

Can I reserve tickets?	**Kann ich Karten vorbestellen?** kän ish kär'tən fōr'bəstelən?
Do you still have tickets for *today/ tomorrow*?	**Haben Sie noch Karten für *heute/ morgen*?** hä'bən zē nōh kär'tən fēr *hoi'tə/môr'gən*?
I'd like *one ticket/two tickets* for …	**Bitte *eine Karte/zwei Karten* für …** bit'ə *i'nə kär'tə/tsvī kär'tən* fēr …
this evening.	**heute Abend.** hoi'tə äbənt.
the matinee.	**die Matinee.** dē mätēnā'.
tomorrow.	**morgen.** môr'gən.
How much is a ticket?	**Wie viel kostet eine Karte?** vē fēl kôs'tət i'nə kär'tə?
Is there a discount for …	**Gibt es eine Ermäßigung für …** gēpt es i'nə ermā'sigōōng fēr …
children?	**Kinder?** kin'dər?
senior citizens?	**Senioren?** senē·ôr'ən?
students?	**Studenten?** shtōōden'tən?

7

Culture and Festivals

act	**der Akt** dār äkt
actor	**der Schauspieler** dār shou'shpēlər
actress	**die Schauspielerin** dē shou'shpēlərin

advance booking	**der Vorverkauf** dār fōr'fərkouf
ballet	**das Ballett** däs bälet'
box office	**die Kasse** dē käs'ə
cabaret	**das Kabarett** däs käbäret'
chamber music	**die Kammermusik** dē käm'ərmōōzēk
choir	**der Chor** dār kōr
circus	**der Zirkus** dār tsir'kōōs
cloakroom	**die Garderobe** dē gärdərō'bə
cloakroom ticket	**die Garderobenmarke** dē gärdərō'bənmär'kə
composer	**der Komponist** dār kômpōnist'
concert	**das Konzert** däs kôntsert'
concert hall	**der Konzertsaal** dār kôntsert'zäl
conductor	**der Dirigent** dār dirigent'
dancer *(male)*	**der Tänzer** dār ten'tsər
dancer *(female)*	**die Tänzerin** dē ten'tsərin
director *(male)*	**der Regisseur** dār rezhisār'
director *(female)*	**die Regisseurin** dē rezhisā'rin
end	**das Ende** däs en'də
feature film	**der Spielfilm** dār shpēl'film
folk dance	**der Volkstanz** dār fôlks'tänts
intermission	**die Pause** dē pou'zə
leading role	**die Hauptrolle** dē houpt'rôlə
movie	**der Film** dār film
movie theater	**das Kino** däs kē'nō
music	**die Musik** dē mōōsēk'

open-air theater	**die Freilichtbühne** dē frī'li<u>sh</u>tbēnə
opening night	**die Premiere** dē premē·ā'rə
opera	**die Oper** dē ō'pər
orchestra	**das Orchester** däs ôrkes'tər
to perform	**aufführen** ouf'fē̅rən
performance	**die Vorstellung** dē fōr'shteloong
play	**das Theaterstück** däs tē·ä'tərshtik
to play	**spielen** shpē'lən
première	**die Premiere** dē premē·ā'rə
production	**die Inszenierung** dē instsānē'rōong
seat	**der Platz** där pläts
set	**das Bühnenbild** däs bē'nənbilt
singer *(male)*	**der Sänger** där zeng'ər
singer *(female)*	**die Sängerin** dē zeng'ərin
soloist *(male)*	**der Solist** där zōlist'
soloist *(female)*	**die Solistin** dē zōlis'tin
start	**der Beginn** där bəgin'
subtitle	**der Untertitel** där ōon'tərtētəl
theater	**das Theater** däs tē·ä'tər
usher *(male)*	**der Platzanweiser** där pläts'änvī̅zər
usher *(female)*	**die Platzanweiserin** dē pläts'änvī̅zərin
variety show	**das Varietee** däs värē·ātā'

7

GOING OUT IN THE EVENING

Is there a nice bar around here?
Gibt es hier eine nette Kneipe?
gēpt es hēr ī'nə net'ə knī'pə?

Where can you go dancing around here?
Wo kann man hier tanzen gehen?
vō kän män hēr tän'tsen gā'ən?

Is this seat taken?
Ist hier noch frei? ist hēr nôḫ frī?

Do you serve meals?
Kann man hier auch etwas essen?
kän män hēr ouḫ et'väs es'ən?

I'd like a *beer/glass of wine*, please.
Ein *Bier/Glas Wein*, bitte.
īn bēr/gläs vīn, bit'ə.

The same again, please.
Das Gleiche noch einmal, bitte.
däs glī'ḫə nôḫ īn'mäl, bit'ə.

What would you like to drink?
Was *möchten Sie/möchtest du* trinken? väs meḫ'tən zē/meḫ'tast dōō tring'kən?

Can I buy you …?
Darf ich *Sie/dich* zu … einladen? därf iṣh zē/diṣh tsōō … īn'lädən?

Would you like to dance?
Hätten Sie/Hättest du Lust zu tanzen? het'ən zē/het'əst dōō lōōst tsōō tän'tsən?

188

Post Office and Bank

POST, TELEGRAMS, TELEPHONE

INFO The activities of European post offices are far broader in scope than they are in the United States. In addition to all the usual mail services, the post office is also the telegraph and telephone company, and provides full banking services, including checking and savings accounts. They will also hold mail for travelers. Simply tell your correspondents to write you "Postlagernd" [pôst'lägərnt] in the city of your destination.

Letters and Parcels

Where is the nearest mailbox/post office?	**Wo ist *der nächste Briefkasten/das nächste Postamt?*** vō ist dār näzh'stə brēf'kästən/däs näzh'stə pôst'ämt?
How much is the postage for a *letter/postcard* to the U.S.?	**Was kostet *ein Brief/eine Karte* nach Amerika?** väs kôs'tət i'n brēf/i'nə kär'tə näkh ämä'rikä?
Five ... stamps, please.	**Fünf Briefmarken zu ..., bitte.** fŭnf brēf'märkən tsōō ..., bit'ə.
Do you have any commemorative issues?	**Haben Sie auch Sondermarken?** hä'bən zē ouh zôn'dərmärkən?

I'd like to mail this letter/package …, please.	**Ich möchte *diesen Brief/dieses Päckchen* bitte … aufgeben.** ish meshʹtə dēʹzən brēf/dēʹzəs pekʹshən bitʹə … oufʹgābən.

registered	**per Einschreiben** per inʹshrībən
airmail	**per Luftpost** per lŏŏftʹpôst
surface mail	**per Seepost** per zāʹpôst

Where is the general delivery counter?	**Wo ist der Schalter für postlagernde Sendungen?** vōō ist dār shälʹtər fēr pôstʹlägərndə zenʹdōōngən?

Is there any mail for me?	**Haben Sie Post für mich?** häʹbən zē pôst fēr mish?

8

The Line Home

INFO You can direct-dial North America from almost any telephone in Europe. The country code for the U.S. and Canada is 001, followed, of course, by the area code and the subscriber's number. You will need operator assistance for person-to-person or collect calls.

Where can I make a phone call?	**Wo kann ich hier telefonieren?** vō kän ish hēr tālāfōnēʹrən?

| Excuse me, could you give me some change to make a phone call? | **Entschuldigung, können Sie mir Kleingeld zum Telefonieren geben?** entshōōl'digōōng, kĕn'ən zē mēr klin'gelt tsōōm tālāfōnē'rən gā'bən? | |

| How much does a 3-minute call to the U.S. cost? | **Was kostet ein 3-minütiges Gespräch nach Amerika?** väs kôs'tət īn drī-minē'tigəs gəshprāsh' näh āmā'rikä? | |

| What's the area code for …? | **Wie ist die Vorwahl von …?** vē ist dē fōr'väl fōn …? | |

	Die Leitung ist *besetzt/gestört*.	The line is *busy/out of order.*
•	dē lī'tōōng ist bəzetst'/gəshtārt'.	

	Es meldet sich niemand.	There's no answer at that number.
•	es mel'dət zish nē'mänt.	

INFO In Germany Telecom used to have a monopoly in the telephone stakes. Now, however, there is a whole range of private telephone companies each offering their own rates and special deals. Making a phone call has, for the most part, become cheaper but also more complicated due to the varying rates on offer. If you wish to phone the U.S. it is worthwhile enquiring about the various rates different companies offer – by doing so you will most certainly save some precious holiday money.

A further tip on how to save money: don't make a call from your hotel room as you will be charged at a much higher rate. Use a public phone booth or go to a post office.

Code Alphabet

A	Anton [än'tōn]	**L** Ludwig [lōōt'vish]	**U** Ulrich [ōōl'rish]
B	Berta [ber'tä]	**M** Martha [märʹtä]	**V** Viktor [vik'tōr]
C	Cäsar [tsä'zär]	**N** Nordpol [nôrt'pōl]	**W** Wilhelm [vil'helm]
D	Dora [dō'rä]		
E	Emil [ā'mēl]	**O** Otto [ôt'ō]	**X** Xaver [ksä'vər]
F	Friedrich [frēd'rish]	**P** Paula [pou'lä]	**Y** Ypsilon [ip'silôn]
G	Georg [gā'ôrk]	**Q** Quelle [kvel'ə]	**Z** Zeppelin [tsep'əlēn]
H	Heinrich [hīn'rish]	**R** Richard [rish'ärt]	**Ä** Ärger [er'gər]
I	Ida [ē'dä]	**S** Samuel [zä'mōō-äl]	**Ö** Ökonom [ākōnōm']
J	Johann [yō'hän]	**T** Theodor [tā'ōdōr]	**Ü** Übermut [ē'bərmōōt]
K	Kaufmann [kouf'män]		

Post, Telegrams, Telephone

address	**die Adresse**	dē ädres'ə
addressee	**der Empfänger**	dār empfeng'ər
airmail	**die Luftpost**	dē lōōft'pôst
area code	**die Vorwahl**	dē fōr'väl
busy	**besetzt**	bezetst'

by airmail	**per Luftpost** per lōōft'pôst
charge	**die Gebühr** dē gəbēr'
charge-card phone	**das Kartentelefon** däs kär'təntālāfōn'
COD	**die Nachnahme** dē näh'nämə
collect call	**das R-Gespräch** däs er'geshprä_sh_
to connect	**verbinden** fərbin'dən
counter	**der Schalter** där shäl'tər
customs declaration	**die Zollerklärung** dē tsôl'erklā'rōōng
declaration of value	**die Wertangabe** dē värt'ängä'bə
discount rate	**der Nachttarif** där nä_sht_'tärēf
express letter	**der Eilbrief** där īl'brēf
fax	**das Telefax** däs tā'ləfäks
general delivery	**postlagernd** pôst'lägərnt
international call	**das Auslandsgespräch**
	däs ous'länstgəshprä_sh_'
letter	**der Brief** där brēf
to mail	**aufgeben** ouf'gābən
mailbox	**der Briefkasten** där brēf'kästən
to make a phone call	**telefonieren** tālāfōnē'rən
package	**das Paket** däs päkät'
parcel ID form	**die Paketkarte** dē päkät'kärtə
payphone	**das Münztelefon** däs mintz'tālāfōn'
picture postcard	**die Ansichtskarte** dē än'zi_sh_tskär'tə
post office	**das Postamt** däs pôst'ämt
to put *(someone)* through	**durchstellen** dōōr_sh_'shtelən

194

registered package	**das Wertpaket** däs vārt'päkāt
to send	**schicken** shik'ən
sender	**der Absender** dār äp'sendər
small package	**das Päckchen** däs pek'shən
stamp	**die Briefmarke** dē brēf'märkə
stamp-vending machine	**der Briefmarkenautomat** dār brēf'märkənoutōmät
telegram	**das Telegramm** däs tālāgräm'
telephone	**das Telefon** däs tālāfōn'
telephone booth	**die Telefonzelle** dē tālāfōn'tselə
telephone directory	**das Telefonbuch** däs tālāfōn'bōōh
telephone exchange	**die Vermittlung** dē fərmit'lōōng

8

MONEY MATTERS

German Marks (DM) – DM 1 = 100 Pf (Pfennig [pfen'ish]),

Austrian Schillings (ATS) –

ATS 1 = 100 g (Groschen [grôsh'ən]),

Swiss Francs (SFR) –

SFR 1 = 100 Ct./Rp. (Centimes [säNtēm']/Rappen [räp'ən])

Where can I exchange some foreign money?	**Wo kann ich Geld wechseln?** vō kän ish gelt vek'səln?

What's the commission charge?	**Wie hoch sind die Gebühren?**	vē hōh zint dē gəbē̄'rən?
What time does the bank close?	**Wie lange ist die Bank geöffnet?**	vē läng'ə ist dē bängk gə·ef'nət?
I'd like to change … dollars into	**Ich möchte … Dollar in … umtauschen.**	ish mesh'tə … dôl'är in … ōōm'toushən.

> German marks **DM** dä'märk
>
> Austrian shillings **Schilling** shil'ing
>
> Swiss francs **Schweizer Franken** shvī'tsər fräng'kən

Can I use my credit card to get cash?	**Kann ich mit meiner Kreditkarte Bargeld bekommen?**	kän ish mit mī'nər krädēt'kärtə bär'gelt bəkôm'ən?
I'd like to cash a traveler's check.	**Ich möchte einen Reisescheck einlösen.**	ish mesh'tə ī'nən rī'zəshek īn'lāzən.

! **Unterschreiben Sie bitte hier.**	ōōntərshrī'bən zē bit'ə hēr.	Would you sign here, please.

? **Wie möchten Sie das Geld haben?**	vē mesh'tən zē däs gelt hä'bən?	How would you like the money?

In small bills, please.	**In kleinen Scheinen, bitte.** in klī'nən shī'nən, bit'ə.

Opening hours for banks vary slightly. The following times can be used as a general guide:

Mon, Tues, Wed, Fri: 9 am to 12.30 and from 1.30 pm to 3.30 pm

Thurs: 9 am to 12.30 and from 1.30 pm to 5.30 pm

Sat: closed all day

In addition to this many banks have cash points where you can withdraw money using your credit card and PIN number.

Money Matters

amount	**der Betrag** dār bəträk'
ATM	**der Geldautomat** dār gelt'outōmät
bank	**die Bank** dē bängk
bank account	**das Bankkonto** däs bäng'kónto
bill	**der Geldschein** dār gelt'shīn
cash	**bar** bär
cash	**das Bargeld** däs bär'gelt
change	**das Kleingeld** däs klīn'gelt
to change	**wechseln** vek'səln
check	**der Scheck** dār shek
coin	**die Münze** dē mĭn'tsə
commission	**die Gebühr** dē gəbēr'
counter	**der Schalter** dār shäl'tər
credit card	**die Kreditkarte** dē krädēt'kärtə
currency	**die Währung** dē vā'rōōng
to deposit	**einzahlen** īn'tsälən

8

deutschmark	**die D-Mark** dē dā'märk
to exchange	**wechseln** vek'səln
exchange rate	**der Kurs** dār kŏŏrs
to have money wired	**telegrafisch Geld überweisen lassen**
	tālāgrä'fish gelt ēbərvī'zən läs'ən
money	**das Geld** däs gelt
payment	**die Zahlung** dē tsä'lŏŏng
receipt	**die Quittung** dē kvit'ŏŏng
shilling	**der Schilling** dār shil'ing
to sign	**unterschreiben** ŏŏntərshrī'bən
signature	**die Unterschrift** dē ŏŏn'tərshrift
Swiss franc	**der Schweizer Franken**
	dār shvī'tsər fräng'kən
transfer	**die Überweisung** dē ēbərvī'zŏŏng
traveler's check	**der Reisescheck** dār rī'zəshek
to withdraw	**abheben** äp'hābən

Emergencies

HEALTH

Information

Could you recommend ...?	**Können Sie mir ... empfehlen?** kœn'ən zē mēr ... empfā'lən?
a lady gynecologist	**eine Frauenärztin** ī'nə frou'ənertstin
a general practitioner	**einen praktischen Arzt** ī'nən präk'tishən ärtst
a dentist	**einen Zahnarzt** ī'nən tsän'ärtst
What are *his/her* office hours?	**Wann hat *er/sie* Sprechstunde?** vän hät är/zē shpresh'shtŏŏndə?
Can *he/she* come here?	**Kann *er/sie* herkommen?** kän är/zē här'kômən?
My *husband/wife* is sick.	***Mein Mann/Meine Frau* ist krank.** *mīn männ/mī'nə frou* ist krängk.
Please call *an ambulance/a doctor*!	**Rufen Sie bitte einen *Krankenwagen/ Notarzt*!** rōō'fən zē bit'ə ī'nən *kräng'kənvägən/nōt'ärtst*!
Where are you taking *him/her*?	**Wohin bringen Sie *ihn/sie*?** vōhin' bring'ən zē *ēn/zē*?

200

| I'd like to come along. | **Ich möchte mitkommen.** ish mesh'tə |
| | mit'kômən. |

Where's the nearest	**Wo ist die nächste Apotheke (mit**
(24-hour) pharmacy?	**Nachtdienst)?** vō ist dē näsh'stə
	äpōtā'kə (mit näht'dēnst)?

Drugstore

| Do you have anything | **Haben Sie etwas gegen …?** hä'bən |
| for …? | zē et'väs gā'gən …? |

| How should I take it? | **Wie muss ich es einnehmen?** vē mōōs |
| | ish es in'nāmən? |

| I need this medicine. | **Ich brauche dieses Medikament.** ish |
| | brou'hə dē'zəs mādikäment'. |

! **Dieses Medikament ist rezept-**	You need a prescrip-
pflichtig. dē'zəs mādikäment' ist	tion for this medicine.
rātsept'pflishtish.	

9

Patient package insert

nach Anweisung des Arztes näh	according to your
än'vīzōōng des ärts'təs	physician's recommen-
	dation

**nach dem Essen im Munde zer-
gehen lassen** näḫ dām es'ən im
mōōn'də tsergä'ən läs'ən

after meals allow to
dissolve in the mouth

vor dem Essen fōr dām es'ən

before meals

äußerlich oi'sərliḫ

external

innerlich in'ərliḫ

internal

auf nüchternen Magen ouf
niṣḥ'tərnən mä'gən

on an empty stomach

rektal rektäl´

rectally

Nebenwirkungen nā'bənvir`kōōngən

side effects

dreimal täglich drī'mäl täg'liṣḥ

three times a day

unzerkaut ōōn'tserkout

whole

Drugstore

antacid	**die Magentabletten** *(plural)* dē mä'gəntäblet`ən
anti-itch cream	**die Salbe gegen Juckreiz** dē zäl'bə gā'gən yōōk'rīts
antibiotic	**das Antibiotikum** däs än`tēbē-ō'ti-kōōm
antiseptic ointment	**die Wundsalbe** dē vōōnt'sälbə
antiseptic solution	**die Desinfektionslösung** dē des`-infektsyōns'lā̧zōōng
aspirins	**die Kopfschmerztabletten** *(plural)* dē kôpf'shmertstäblet`ən

chamomile tea	**der Kamillentee** dār kämil'əntā
charcoal tablets	**die Kohletabletten** dē kō'lətäblet'ən
circulatory stimulant	**das Kreislaufmittel** däs krīs'loufmit'əl
condom	**das Kondom** däs kôndō'm
contraceptive pill	**die Antibabypille** dē än'tēbā'bēpilə
cotton	**die Watte** dē vät'ə
cough syrup	**der Hustensaft** dār hōōs'tənzäft
drops	**die Tropfen** *(plural)* dē trôp'fən
elastic bandage	**die Elastikbinde** dē äläs'tikbin'də
first-aid kit	**das Verbandszeug** däs fərbän'tsoik
gauze bandage	**die Mullbinde** dē mōōl'bində
homeopathic	**homöopathisch** hō'mə̄-ōpä'tish
insulin	**das Insulin** däs inzōōlēn'
iodine	**das Jod** däs yōt
laxative	**das Abführmittel** däs äp'fē̇rmit'əl
medicine	**das Medikament** däs mādikämänt'
night duty	**der Nachtdienst** dār näh'dēnst
ointment	**die Salbe** dē zäl'bə
ointment for mosquito bites	**die Salbe gegen Mückenstiche** dē zäl'bə gä'gən mik'ənshtishə
ointment for sun allergy	**die Salbe gegen Sonnenallergie** dē zäl'bə gä'gən zôn'ənälərgē'
ointment for sunburn	**die Salbe gegen Sonnenbrand** dē zäl'bə gä'gən zôn'ənbränt
painkiller	**das Schmerzmittel** däs shmerts'mitəl
pharmacy	**die Apotheke** dē äpōtā'kə

9

pill	**die Pille** dē pil'ə
powder	**der Puder** dār pōō'dər
prescription	**das Rezept** däs rātsept'
prescription medicine	**das rezeptpflichtige Mittel** däs rātsept'pflis̲h̲'tigə mit'əl
sanitary napkin	**die Damenbinde** dē dä'mənbində
sleeping pills	**die Schlaftabletten** *(plural)* dē shläf'täblet'ən
something for ...	**ein Mittel gegen ...** īn mit'əl gā'gən ...
suppository	**das Zäpfchen** däs tsepf's̲h̲en
tablet	**die Tablette** dē täblet'ə
tampons	**die Tampons** *(plural)* dē täm'pôns
thermometer	**das Fieberthermometer** däs fē'bər-tārmōmā'tər
throat lozenges	**die Halsschmerztabletten** *(plural)* dē häls'shmertstäblet'ən
tranquilizer	**das Beruhigungsmittel** däs bərōō'igōōngsmit'əl

At the Doctor's

| I have a (bad) cold. | **Ich bin (stark) erkältet.** is̲h̲ bin (shtärk) erkel'tət. |
| I have *diarrhea/a (high) fever.* | **Ich habe *Durchfall/(hohes) Fieber.*** is̲h̲ hä'bə *dōōrs̲h̲'fäl/(hō'əs) fē'bər.* |

204

I don't feel well.	**Ich fühle mich nicht wohl.** i<u>sh</u> fē'lə mi<u>sh</u> ni<u>sh</u>t vōl.
My ... hurts/hurt.	**Mir tut/tun ... weh.** mēr tōōt/tōōn ... vā.
I have pains here.	**Hier habe ich Schmerzen.** hēr hä'bə i<u>sh</u> shmer'tsən.
I've been vomiting several times.	**Ich habe mich mehrmals übergeben.** i<u>sh</u> hä'bə mi<u>sh</u> (mār'mäls) ēbərgā'bən.
My stomach is upset.	**Ich habe mir den Magen verdorben.** i<u>sh</u> hä'bə mēr dān mä'gən ferdôr'bən.
I can't move ...	**Ich kann ... nicht bewegen.** i<u>sh</u> kän ... ni<u>sh</u>t bəvā'gən.
I've hurt myself.	**Ich habe mich verletzt.** i<u>sh</u> hä'bə mi<u>sh</u> ferletst'.
I've been *stung/bitten* by ...	**Ich bin von ... gestochen/gebissen worden.** i<u>sh</u> bin fôn ... *gəshtô<u>h</u>'ən/gəbis'ən* vôr'dən.

9

I have (not) been vaccinated against …	**Ich bin (nicht) gegen … geimpft.** i<u>sh</u> bin (ni<u>sh</u>t) gä'gən … ge-impft'.
My last tetanus shot was about … years ago.	**Meine letzte Tetanusimpfung war vor ca. … Jahren.** mī'nə lets'tə tāt'änōōs-im'pfŏŏng vär för tsir'kä … yä'rən.
I'm allergic to penicillin.	**Ich bin allergisch gegen Penizillin.** i<u>sh</u> bin äler'gish gä'gən pen'itsilēn'.
I'm *diabetic/HIV-positive.*	**Ich bin *Diabetiker/HIV-positiv.*** i<u>sh</u> bin dē-äbā'tikər/hä'-ē-fou' pō'sitēv.
I take these tablets regularly.	**Ich nehme diese Tabletten regelmäßig.** i<u>sh</u> nä'mə dē'zə täblet'ən rā'gəlmäsi<u>sh</u>.
I have …	**Ich habe …** i<u>sh</u> hä'bə …
high blood pressure.	**einen hohen Blutdruck.** i'nən hō'ən blōōt'drŏŏk.
low blood pressure.	**einen niedrigen Blutdruck.** i'nən nēd'rigən blōōt'drŏŏk.
a pacemaker.	**einen Herzschrittmacher.** i'nən herts'shritmä<u>h</u>ər.
I'm … months pregnant.	**Ich bin im …ten Monat schwanger.** i<u>sh</u> bin im …tən mō'nät shvängʹər.

What the doctor says

Wo haben Sie Schmerzen? vō hä'bən zē shmer'tsən?	Where does it hurt?
Tut das weh? toot däs vā?	Does that hurt?
Öffnen Sie bitte den Mund. ef'nən zē bit'ə dān mōōnt.	Open your mouth, please.
Zeigen Sie bitte die Zunge. tsī'gən zē bit'ə dē tsōōng'ə.	Show me your tongue, please.
Bitte machen Sie *sich/den Oberkörper* **frei.** bit'ə mäh'ən zē *zish/dān* ō'bərkərpər frī.	Would you *get undressed/strip down to the waist*, please.
Bitte machen Sie den Arm frei. bit'ə mäh'ən zē dān ärm frī.	Would you roll up your sleeve, please.
Atmen Sie tief. Atem anhalten. ät'mən zē tēf. ä'təm än'hältən.	Breathe deeply. Hold your breath.
Wie lange haben Sie diese Beschwerden? vē läng'ə hä'bən zē dē'zə bəshvār'dən?	How long have you felt this way?
Sind Sie gegen … geimpft? zint zē gā'gən … gə·impft'?	Have you been vaccinated against …?

9

Wir müssen Sie röntgen. vēr mĭs'ən zē rĕnt'gən.	We need to take some X-rays.
... ist *gebrochen/verstaucht*. ... ist gəbrôh'ən/fershtou̱ht'.	... is *broken/sprained*.
Ich brauche eine *Blutprobe/Urinprobe*. ish brou'hə ī'nə blōōt'prōbə/ōōrēn'prōbə.	I need a *blood/urine* sample.
Sie müssen operiert werden. zē mĭs'ən ôperērt' vār'dən.	You'll have to have an operation.
Ich muß Sie an einen Facharzt überweisen. ish mōōs zē än ī'nən fäh'ärtst ēbərvī'zən.	I need to refer you to a specialist.
Sie brauchen einige Tage Bettruhe. zē brou'hən ī'nigə tä'gə bet'rōō·ə.	You need a few days of bedrest.
Es ist nichts Ernstes. es ist nĭshts ern'stəs.	It's nothing serious.
Nehmen Sie davon dreimal täglich zwei Tabletten. nā'mən zē dä'fôn drī'mäl tāgl'lish tsvī täblet'ən.	Take two tablets three times a day.
Kommen Sie *morgen/in ... Tagen* wieder. kôm'ən zē môr'gən/in ... tä'gən vē'dər.	Come back *tomorrow/ in ... days*.

Can you give me a doctor's certificate?	**Können Sie mir ein Attest ausstellen?** kĕn'ən zē mēr in ặtest' ous'shtelən?
Do I have to come back?	**Muss ich noch einmal kommen?** mōōs ish nôh īn'mäl kôm'ən?
Could you give me a receipt for my medical insurance?	**Geben Sie mir bitte eine Quittung für meine Versicherung.** gā'bən zē mēr bit'ə i'nə kvit'ōōng fēr mi'nə ferzish'ərōōng.

In the Hospital

Is there anyone here who speaks English?	**Gibt es hier jemanden, der Englisch spricht?** gēpt es hēr yā'mändən, dār eng'lish shprisht?
I'd like to speak to a doctor.	**Ich möchte mit einem Arzt sprechen.** ish mesh'tə mit i'nəm ärtst shpresh'ən.
What's the diagnosis?	**Wie lautet die Diagnose?** vē lou'tət dē dē·ägnō'zə?
I'd rather have the operation in the United States.	**Ich möchte mich lieber in Amerika operieren lassen.** ish mesh'tə mish lē'bər in ämä'rikä ôperē'rən läs'ən.

9

209

Would you please notify my family?	**Würden Sie bitte meine Familie benachrichtigen?** vir'dən zē bitə mī'nə fämē'lē·ə bənäh'ri̱shtigən?
Can I have a private room?	**Kann ich ein Einzelzimmer bekommen?** kän i̱sh īn īn'tsəltsimər bəkôm'ən?
When can I get out of bed?	**Wann darf ich aufstehen?** vän därf i̱sh ouf'shtā·ən?
Could you give me *something for the pain/ to get to sleep?*	**Können Sie mir bitte etwas *gegen die Schmerzen/zum Einschlafen geben?*** kɛn'ən zē mēr bit'ə et'väs gā'gən dē shmer'tsən/tsōōm īn'shläfən gā'bən?
I'd like to be discharged (at my own risk).	**Bitte entlassen Sie mich (auf eigene Verantwortung).** bit'ə entläs'ən zē mi̱sh (ouf ī'gənə feränt'vôrtōōng).

Parts of the Body and Organs

abdomen	**der Unterleib** där ōōn'tərlīp
ankle	**der Knöchel** där knesh'əl
appendix	**der Blinddarm** där blint'därm
arm	**der Arm** där ärm
back	**der Rücken** där ri̱k'ən
bladder	**die Blase** dē blä'zə

blood pressure	**der Blutdruck** dār blōōt'drōōk
body	**der Körper** dār ker'pər
bone	**der Knochen** dār knôḫ'ən
bottom	**das Gesäß** dās gəzās'
breast	**die Brust** dē brōōst
bronchial tubes	**die Bronchien** *(plural)* dē brôn'shē·ən
bruise	**der blaue Fleck** dār blou'ə flek
calf	**die Wade** dē vä'də
cheek	**die Wange** dē väng'ə
chest	**der Brustkorb** dār brōōst'kôrp
chin	**das Kinn** dās kin
collarbone	**das Schlüsselbein** dās shlis'əlbīn
disk	**die Bandscheibe** dē bänt'shībə
ear	**das Ohr** dās ōr
eardrum	**das Trommelfell** dās trôm'əlfel
elbow	**der Ellbogen** dār el'bōgən
eye	**das Auge** dās ou'gə
face	**das Gesicht** dās gəzisht'
finger	**der Finger** dār fing'ər
fingernail	**der Fingernagel** dār fing'ərnägəl
foot	**der Fuß** dār fōōs
forehead	**die Stirn** dē shtirn
gall bladder	**die Galle** dē gäl'ə
genitals	**die Geschlechtsorgane** *(plural)* dē gəshlesh̲ts'ôrgä'nə
hand	**die Hand** dē hänt

9

211

head	**der Kopf** dār kôpf	
heart	**das Herz** däs herts	
heel	**die Ferse** dē fer'zə	
hip	**die Hüfte** dē hĭf'tə	
intestine	**der Darm** dār därm	
joint	**das Gelenk** däs gəlengk'	
kidney	**die Niere** dē nē'rə	
knee	**das Knie** däs knē	
kneecap	**die Kniescheibe** dē knē'shībə	
larynx	**der Kehlkopf** dār kāl'kôpf	
leg	**das Bein** däs bīn	
lip	**die Lippe** dē lip'ə	
liver	**die Leber** dē lā'bər	
lower jaw	**der Unterkiefer** dār ōōn'tərkēfər	
lower leg	**der Unterschenkel** dār ōōn'tərshengkəl	
lungs	**die Lunge** dē lōōng'ə	
mouth	**der Mund** dār mōōnt	
muscle	**der Muskel** dār mōōs'kəl	
neck	**der Hals** dār häls	
nerve	**der Nerv** dār nerf	
nose	**die Nase** dē nä'zə	
pelvis	**das Becken** däs bek'ən	
penis	**der Penis** dār pā'nis	
rib	**die Rippe** dē rip'ə	
rib cage	**der Brustkorb** dār brōōst'kôrp	
shinbone	**das Schienbein** däs shēn'bīn	

shoulder	**die Schulter** dē shŏŏl'tər
shoulder blade	**das Schulterblatt** däs shŏŏl'tərblät
sinus	**die Stirnhöhle** dē shtirn'hālə
skin	**die Haut** dē hout
spine	**die Wirbelsäule** dē vir'bəlzoilə
stomach	**der Magen** där mä'gən
temple	**die Schläfe** dē shlā'fə
tendon	**die Sehne** dē zā'nə
testicles	**die Hoden** *(plural)* dē hō'dən
thigh	**der Oberschenkel** där ō'bərshengkel
throat	**der Rachen** där räh'ən
thumb	**der Daumen** där dou'mən
thyroid gland	**die Schilddrüse** dē shilt'drēzə
toe	**die Zehe** dē tsā'ə
toenail	**der Zehennagel** där tsā'ənägəl
tongue	**die Zunge** dē tsōōng'ə
tonsils	**die Mandeln** *(plural)* dē män'dəln
tooth	**der Zahn** där tsän
upper body	**der Oberkörper** där ō'bərkerpər
upper jaw	**der Oberkiefer** där ō'bərkēfər
vagina	**die Scheide** dē shī'də
vertebra	**der Wirbel** där vir'bəl
wrist	**das Handgelenk** däs hänt'gəlengk

9

AIDS	**das Aids** däs eēdz
allergy	**die Allergie** dē älərgē'
alternative practitioner	**der Heilpraktiker** dār hīl'präk`tikər
appendicitis	**die Blinddarmentzündung** dē blint'därmentsin`dōong
asthma	**das Asthma** däs äst'mä
bee sting	**der Bienenstich** dār bē'nənshti<u>sh</u>
bite	**der Biss** dār bis; *(insect)* **der Stich** dār shti<u>sh</u>
bleeding	**die Blutung** dē blōō'tōōng
blister	**die Blase** dē blä'zə
blood	**das Blut** däs blōōt
blood poisoning	**die Blutvergiftung** dē blōōt'fərgiftōōng
blood pressure	**der Blutdruck** dār blōōt'drōōk
blood test	**die Blutprobe** dē blōōt'prōbə
blood transfusion	**die Bluttransfusion** dē blōōt'tränsfōōzyōn`
blood type	**die Blutgruppe** dē blōōt'grōōpə
boil	**das Furunkel** däs fōōrōōng'kəl
broken	**gebrochen** gəbrô<u>h</u>'ən
bronchitis	**die Bronchitis** dē brôn<u>sh</u>ē'tis
bruise	**die Prellung** dē prel'ōōng
burn	**die Verbrennung** dē fərbren'ōōng

214

certificate	**das Attest** däs ätest'
chicken pox	**die Windpocken** *(plural)* dē vint'pôkən
circulatory problems	**die Kreislaufstörungen** *(plural)* dē krīs'loufshtā'rōōngən
cold	**die Erkältung** dē erkel'tōōng
cold	**der Schnupfen** dār shnōōp'fən
colic	**die Kolik** dē kō'lik
concussion	**die Gehirnerschütterung** dē gəhirn'ərshītərōōng
conjunctivitis	**die Bindehautentzündung** dē bin'dəhoutentsin'dōōng
constipation	**die Verstopfung** dē fərshtôp'fōōng
coronary	**der Herzinfarkt** dār herts'infärkt
cough	**der Husten** dār hōōs'tən
to cough	**husten** hōōs'tən
cramp	**der Krampf** dār krämpf
cut	**die Schnittwunde** dē shnit'vōōndə
cystitis	**die Blasenentzündung** dē blä'zənentsin'dōōng
dermatologist	**der Hautarzt** dār hout'ärtst
diabetes	**der Diabetes** dār dē·abä'tes
diagnosis	**die Diagnose** dē dē·ägnō'zə
diarrhea	**der Durchfall** dār dōōr<u>sh</u>'fäl
to discharge	**entlassen** entläs'ən
disease	**die Krankheit** dē krängk'hīt
dislocated	**verrenkt** verengkt'

9

215

dizziness	**der Schwindel** dār shvin'dəl
doctor	**der Arzt, die Ärztin** dār ärtst, dē erts'tin
ear, nose, and throat doctor	**der Hals-Nasen-Ohren-Arzt** dār häls'-nä'zən-ō'rən-ärtst
to faint	**ohnmächtig werden** ōn'meshtish vär'dən
fever	**das Fieber** däs fē'bər
flu	**die Grippe** dē grip'ə
food poisoning	**die Lebensmittelvergiftung** dē lā'bənsmitəlfərgif'tŏng
fungal infection	**die Pilzinfektion** dē pilts'infektsyōn
gallstones	**die Gallensteine** *(plural)* dē gäl'ənshtīnə
general practitioner	**der praktische Arzt** dār präk'tishə ärtst
German measles	**die Röteln** *(plural)* dē rä'təln
to get out of bed	**aufstehen** ouf'shtā·ən
gynecologist	**der Frauenarzt** dār frou'ənärtst
hay fever	**der Heuschnupfen** dār hoi'shnŏŏpfən
heart	**das Herz** däs herts
heart attack	**der Herzanfall** dār herts'änfäl
heart complaint	**der Herzfehler** dār herts'fālər
hematoma	**der Bluterguss** dār blōōt'ərgŏŏs
hemorrhoids	**die Hämorriden** *(plural)* dē hemôrē'dən
hernia	**der Leistenbruch** dār līs'tənbrŏŏh

herpes	**der Herpes** dār her'pes	
hurt	**verletzt** fərletst'	
illness	**die Krankheit** dē krängk'hīt	
infection	**die Infektion** dē infektsyōn'	
infectious	**ansteckend** än'shtekənt	
inflammation	**die Entzündung** dē entsin'dŏŏng	
internist	**der Internist** dār intərnist'	
kidney stones	**die Nierensteine** *(plural)* dē nē'rənshtīnə	
lumbago	**der Hexenschuss** dār hek'sənshŏŏs	
measles	**die Masern** *(plural)* dē mä'zərn	
meningitis	**die Hirnhautentzündung** dē hirn'- houtentsin`dŏŏng	
menstruation	**die Menstruation** dē men`strŏŏ·ätsē·ōn'	
migraine	**die Migräne** dē migrä'nə	
mumps	**der Mumps** dār mŏŏmps	
nausea	**die Übelkeit** dē ē'bəlkīt	**9**
neuralgia	**die Neuralgie** dē noirälgē'	
nose bleed	**das Nasenbluten** däs nä'zənblŏŏtən	
nurse	**die Krankenschwester** dē kräng'kən- shves'tər	
office hours	**die Sprechstunde** dē shpresh'shtŏŏndə	
to operate	**operieren** ōpərē'rən	
ophthalmologist	**der Augenarzt** dār ou'gənärtst	
orthopedist	**der Orthopäde** dār ôrtōpä'də	

pacemaker	**der Herzschrittmacher** dār herts'- shritmähər
pains	**die Schmerzen** *(plural)* dē shmer'tsən
paralyzed	**gelähmt** gəlämt'
paraplegic	**querschnittgelähmt** kvär'shnitgəlämt'
pediatrician	**der Kinderarzt** dār kin'dərärtst
period	**die Periode** dē pāryō'də
pleurisy	**die Rippenfellentzündung** dē rip'ənfelentsin'dōōng
pneumonia	**die Lungenentzündung** dē lōōng'ənentsin'dōōng
polio	**die Kinderlähmung** dē kin'dərlā'mōōng
pregnant	**schwanger** shväng'ər
to prescribe	**verschreiben** fərshrī'bən
pulled muscle	**die Zerrung** dē tser'ōōng
pus	**der Eiter** dār ī'tər
rash	**der Ausschlag** dār ous'shläk
rheumatism	**das Rheuma** däs roī'mä
scarlet fever	**der Scharlach** dār shär'läh
sciatica	**der Ischias** dār 'ēshē·äs
sexually transmitted disease	**die Geschlechtskrankheit** dē gəshlehts'krängk·hīt
shivering fit	**der Schüttelfrost** dār shit'əlfrôst
shock	**der Schock** dār shôk
to have a sore throat	**Halsschmerzen haben** häls'shmertsən hä'bən

sprained	**verstaucht** fərshtou<u>h</u>t'
stomach ulcer	**das Magengeschwür** däs mä'gəngəshvēr
stomach-ache	**die Magenschmerzen** *(plural)* dē mä'gənshmertsən
stroke	**der Schlaganfall** dār shläg'änfäl
sunburn	**der Sonnenbrand** dār zôn'ənbränt
sweat	**der Schweiß** dār shvīs
swelling	**die Schwellung** dē shvel'ōōng
to have a temperature	**Fieber haben** fē'bər hä'bən
tetanus	**der Tetanus** dār tet'änōōs
thrush	**der Ausschlag** dār ous'shläk
tonsillitis	**die Mandelentzündung** dē män'dəlentsin'dōōng
torn ligament	**der Bänderriss** dār ben'dəris
travel sickness	**die Reisekrankheit** dē rī'zəkrängk·hīt
ulcer	**das Geschwür** däs gəshvēr'
urologist	**der Urologe** dār ōōrōlō'gə
vaccination	**die Impfung** dē im'pfōōng
vomiting	**das Erbrechen** däs erbresh'ən
ward	**die Station** dē shtätsyōn'
wasp sting	**der Wespenstich** dār ves'pənshti<u>sh</u>
whooping cough	**der Keuchhusten** dār koi<u>sh</u>'hōōstən
to X-ray	**röntgen** rent'gən

9

At the Dentist's

This tooth ... hurts.	**Der Zahn ... tut weh.** där tsän ... tōōt vä.
back here	**hier hinten** hēr hin'tən
at the top	**oben** ō'bən
down here	**hier unten** hēr ōōn'tən
in front	**vorn** fôrn
This tooth has broken off.	**Der Zahn ist abgebrochen.** där tsän ist äp'gəbrôḫən.
I've lost a filling.	**Ich habe eine Füllung verloren.** i<u>sh</u> hä'bə ī'nə fi̱l'ōōng ferlō'rən.
Can you do a temporary job on the tooth?	**Können Sie den Zahn provisorisch behandeln?** ke̱n'ən zē dän tsän prōvēsōr'ish bəhän'dəln?
Please don't pull the tooth.	**Den Zahn bitte nicht ziehen.** dän tsän bit'ə ni<u>sh</u>t tsē'ən.
Would you give me/ I'd rather not have an injection, please.	**Geben Sie mir bitte *eine/keine* Spritze.** gā'bən zē mēr bit'ə *ī'nə/ kī'nə* shprit'sə.
Can you repair these dentures?	**Können Sie diese Prothese reparieren?** ke̱n'ən zē dē'zə prōtä'zə repärē'rən?

Sie brauchen eine ... zē brou'ḫən i'nə ...	You need a ...
Brücke. brĭk'ə.	bridge.
Füllung. fĭl'ōōng.	filling.
Krone. krō'nə.	crown.
Ich muß den Zahn ziehen. iṣh mōōs dān tsän tsē'ən.	I'll have to pull the tooth.
Bitte gut spülen. bĭt'ə gōōt shpē'lən.	Rinse out your mouth, please.

Dentist

amalgam filling	**die Amalgamfüllung** dē ämälgäm'-fĭlōōng
brace(s)	**die Zahnspange** dē tsän'shpängə
bridge	**die Brücke** dē brĭk'ə
caries	**die Karies** dē kär'ē·es
crown	**die Krone** dē krō'nə
dental assistant	**die Zahnarzthelferin** dē tsän'ärtst-hel'ferin
dentist	**der Zahnarzt** dār tsän'ärtst
dentures	**die Prothese** dē prōtā'zə
to extract	**ziehen** tsē'ən
filling	**die Füllung** dē fĭl'ōōng

9

221

gums	**das Zahnfleisch** däs tsän'flīsh
hole	**das Loch** däs lôḫ
inflammation	**die Entzündung** dē entsin'dōōng
injection	**die Spritze** dē shprit'sə
jaw	**der Kiefer** dār kē'fər
local anesthetic	**die Betäubung** dē bətoi'bōōng
neck of the tooth	**der Zahnhals** dār tsän'häls
nerve	**der Nerv** dār nerf
office hours	**die Sprechstunde** dē shpreḫ'shtōōndə
pivot tooth	**der Stiftzahn** dār shtift'tsän
plaque	**der Zahnbelag** dār tsän'bəläk
pyorrhea	**die Parodontose** dē pä'rōdôntō'zə
root-canal work	**die Wurzelbehandlung** dē vōōr'tsəlbəhänd'lōōng
tartar	**der Zahnstein** dār tsän'shtīn
temporary filling	**das Provisorium** däs prōvisōr'ē·ōōm
tooth	**der Zahn** dār tsän
tooth decay	**die Karies** dē kär'ē·es
wisdom tooth	**der Weisheitszahn** dār vīs'hīts·tsän

POLICE; LOST AND FOUND

Where is the nearest police station?	**Wo ist die nächste Polizeiwache?** vō ist dē nāsh'stə pōlitsi'vähə?
Does anyone here speak English?	**Gibt es hier jemanden, der Englisch spricht?** gēpt es hēr yā'mändən, dār eng'lish shprisht?
I'd like to report …	**Ich möchte … anzeigen.** ish mesh'tə … än'tsīgən.
a theft.	**einen Diebstahl** i'nən dēp'shtäl
a mugging.	**einen Überfall** i'nən ē'bərfäl
a rape.	**eine Vergewaltigung** i'nə fergə-väl'tigōōng
My *daughter/son* has disappeared.	***Meine Tochter/Mein Sohn* ist verschwunden.** mī'nə tôh'tər/mīn zōn ist fershvōōn'dən.
My … has been stolen.	**Man hat mir … gestohlen.** män hät mēr … gəshtō'lən.
I've lost …	**Ich habe … verloren.** ish hä'bə … fərlō'rən.
My car has been broken into.	**Mein Auto ist aufgebrochen worden.** mīn ou'tō ist ouf'gəbrôh'ən vôr'dən.

9

My room was burglarized.	**In meinem Zimmer ist eingebrochen worden.** in mī'nəm tsim'ər ist in'gəbrȫən vôr'dən.
I've been *cheated/assaulted.*	**Ich bin *betrogen/zusammengeschlagen* worden.** ish bin bətrō'gən/ tsōōsäm'əngashlä'gən vôr'dən.
I need a copy of the official report for insurance purposes.	**Ich benötige eine Bescheinigung für meine Versicherung.** ish bənə'tigə ī'nə bəshī'nigōōng fēr mī'nə fərzish'ərōōng.
I'd like to speak to my *lawyer/consulate.*	**Ich möchte mit meinem *Anwalt/ Konsulat* sprechen.** ish mesh'tə mit mī'nəm än'vält/kônzōōlät' shpresh'ən.
I'm innocent.	**Ich bin unschuldig.** ish bin ōōn'shōōldish.
That's the *man/woman.*	**Das ist *der Mann/die Frau.*** däs ist där män/dē frou.

What the police say

Füllen Sie bitte dieses Formular aus. fil'ən zē bit'ə dē'zəs fôrmōōlär' ous.	Please fill out this form.
Ihren Pass, bitte. ē'rən päs, bit'ə.	Your passport, please.

224

Wo wohnen Sie *in Amerika/hier?*	What is your address *in the U.S./here?*
vō vō'nən zē *in ämä'rikä/hēr?*	

Wann/Wo ist es passiert?	*When/Where* did this happen?
vän/vō ist es päsērt'?	

Wenden Sie sich bitte an Ihr Konsulat.	Please get in touch with your consulate.
ven'dən zē zi<u>sh</u> bit'ə än ēr kônzōōlät'.	

Police; Lost and found

accident	**der Unfall** dār ōōn'fäl
to arrest	**verhaften** ferhäf'tən
to assault	**zusammenschlagen** tsōōzäm'ən-shlägən
broken into	**aufgebrochen** ouf'gəbrô<u>h</u>ən
car	**das Auto** däs ou'tō
consulate	**das Konsulat** däs kônzōōlät'
drugs	**das Rauschgift** däs roush'gift
form	**das Formular** däs fôrmōōlär'
lawyer	**der Anwalt** dār än'vält
lost	**verloren** ferlō'rən
to molest	**belästigen** beles'tigən
mugging	**der Überfall** dār ē'bərfäl
passport	**der Reisepass** dār rī'zəpäs
pickpocket	**der Taschendieb** dār täsh'əndēp

9

225

police	**die Polizei** dē pōlitsī'
police car	**der Polizeiwagen** dār pōlitsī'vägən
police patrol	**die Polizeistreife** dē pōlitsī'shtrīfə
police station	**die Polizeiwache** dē pōlitsī'vähə
policeofficer	**der Polizist** dār pōlitsist'
purse	**die Handtasche** dē hän'täshə
rape	**die Vergewaltigung** dē fergəvälˈtigoong
to report to the police	**anzeigen** änˈtsīgən
robbery	**der Überfall** dār ē'bərfäl
stolen	**gestohlen** gəshtōˈlən
theft	**der Diebstahl** dār dēp'shtäl
thief	**der Dieb** dār dēp
wallet	**das Portemonnaie** däs pôrtmōnä'
witness	**der Zeuge** dār tsoi'gə

Time and Weather

ZEIT

Time of Day

What time is it?	**Wie spät ist es?** vē shpāt ist es?
It's one o'clock.	**Es ist 1 Uhr.** es ist īn ōōr.
It's twenty-five minutes to four.	**Es ist 15 Uhr 35.** es ist fฺฺฺฺฺฺฺนf'tsān ōōr fฺนf·ōōnt·drī'sis̱h.
It's quarter past five.	**Es ist Viertel nach 5.** es ist vir'tᵊl näẖ fฺนf.
It's six-thirty.	**Es ist halb 7.** es ist hälp zē'bᵊn.
It's quarter to nine.	**Es ist Viertel vor 9.** es ist vir'tᵊl fōr noin.
It's five after four.	**Es ist 5 (Minuten) nach 4.** es ist fฺนf (minōō'tᵊn) näẖ fēr.
It's ten to eight.	**Es ist 10 (Minuten) vor 8.** es ist tsān (minōō'tᵊn) fôr äẖt.
At what time?	**Um wie viel Uhr?** ōōm vē fēl ōōr?
At ten o'clock.	**Um 10 Uhr.** ōōm tsān ōōr.
From eight till nine o'clock.	**Von 8 bis 9 Uhr.** fôn äẖt bis noin.

Between ten and twelve.	**Zwischen 10 und 12 Uhr.** tsvish'ən tsän ōōnt tsvelf ōōr.	
Not before seven p.m.	**Nicht vor 19 Uhr.** nisht fōr noin'tsän ōōr.	
In half an hour.	**In einer halben Stunde.** in i'nər häl'bən shtōōn'də.	
It's too late.	**Es ist (zu) spät.** es ist (tsōō) shpāt.	
It's still too early.	**Es ist noch zu früh.** es ist nôh tsōō frē.	
Is your watch right?	**Geht Ihre Uhr richtig?** gāt ē'rə ōōr rish'tish?	
It's *fast/slow*.	**Sie geht *vor/nach*.** zē gāt fōr/näh.	

Basic Vocabulary

afternoon	**Nachmittag** näh'mitäk	
... ago	**vor ...** fōr	
a month ago	**vor einem Monat** fōr i'nəm mō'nät	
at night	**nachts** nähts	
at noon today	**heute Mittag** hoi'tə mit'äk	
at midday	**mittags** mit'äks	
at the moment	**zur Zeit** tsōōr tsit	
before	**vorher** fōr'hār	
day	**der Tag** där täk	
earlier	**früher** frē'ər	

10

early	**früh** frē
evening	**der Abend** dār ä'bənt
every day	**täglich** tāk'li̱sh
every hour	**stündlich** shtĭnt'li̱sh
every week	**jede Woche** yā'də vô̱h'ə
for ten days	**seit zehn Tagen** zīt tsān tä'gən
for the time being	**vorläufig** fōr'loifi̱sh
from time to time	**von Zeit zu Zeit** fôn tsīt tsōō tsīt
half an hour	**eine halbe Stunde** ī'nə hạl'bə shtōōn'də
hour	**die Stunde** dē shtōōn'də
in a week	**in einer Woche** in ī'nər vô̱h'ə
in the afternoon	**nachmittags** nä̱h'mitäks
in the evening	**abends** ä'bənts
in the morning	**morgens, vormittags** môr'gəns, fōr'mitäks
in two weeks	**in 14 Tagen** in fir'tzān tä'gən
in time	**rechtzeitig** re̱sh'tsīti̱sh
last night	**heute Nacht** hoi'tə nä̱ht
last year	**voriges Jahr** fōr'igəs yär
late	**spät** shpät
later	**später** shpät'ər
minute	**die Minute** dē minōō'tə
month	**der Monat** dār mō'nät
morning	**der Morgen** dār môr'gən
next year	**nächstes Jahr** nä̱sh'stəs yär

night	**die Nacht** dē nä<u>h</u>t
now	**jetzt** yetst
on the weekend	**am Wochenende** äm vô<u>h</u>'ənendə
a quarter of an hour	**eine Viertelstunde** i'nə firtəlshtōon'də
recently	**vor kurzem** fōr kōōr'tsəm
second	**die Sekunde** dē zekōōn'də
since	**seit** zīt
six months	**ein halbes Jahr** īn häl'bəs yär
sometimes	**manchmal** män<u>sh</u>'mäl
soon	**bald** bält
the day after tomorrow	**übermorgen** ē'bərmôrgən
the day before yesterday	**vorgestern** fōr'gestərn
this afternoon	**heute Nachmittag** hoi'tə nä<u>h</u>'mitäk
this evening	**heute Abend** hoi'tə ä'bənt
this morning	**heute Morgen** hoi'tə môr'gən
time	**die Zeit** dē tsīt
today	**heute** hoi'tə
tomorrow	**morgen** môr'gən
until	**bis** bis
week	**die Woche** dē vô<u>h</u>'ə
within a week	**innerhalb einer Woche** in'ərhälp ī'nər vô<u>h</u>'ə
year	**das Jahr** däs yär
yesterday	**gestern** ges'tərn

10

The seasons

fall	**der Herbst** dār herpst
spring	**der Frühling** dār frē'ling
summer	**der Sommer** dār zôm'ər
winter	**der Winter** dār vin'tər

INFO Summertime is from the end of March to the end of October, i.e. clocks are put forward an hour the last weekend in March during the night between Saturday and Sunday. On the last Saturday to Sunday night in October the process is reversed and clocks are put back an hour.

Legal Holidays

Christmas Eve	**Heiligabend** hīlishä'bənt
Christmas	**Weihnachten** vī'nähtən
New Year	**Neujahr** noi'yär
New Year's Eve	**Silvester** zilves'tər
Epiphany	**Heilige Drei Könige** hī'ligə drī kā'nigə
Good Friday	**Karfreitag** kärfrī'täk
Easter	**Ostern** ō'stərn
May Day	**der Erste Mai** dār ārs'tə mī
Ascension Day	**Christi Himmelfahrt** kris'tē him'əlfärt
Whitsun	**Pfingsten** pfing'stən
Corpus Christi	**Fronleichnam** frōnlish'näm

232

Day of the Fall of the Berlin Wall	**Tag der deutschen Einheit** täk dər doit'shən īn'hīt
All Saint's Day	**Allerheiligen** äˌlərhī'ligən

THE DATE

What's today's date?	**Den Wievielten haben wir heute?** dān vē'fēltən hä'bən vēr hoi'tə?
Today is the 2nd of July.	**Heute ist der 2. Juli.** hoi'tə ist dār tsvī'tə yōō'lē.
I was born on the 24th of August, 19...	**Ich bin am 24. August 19.. geboren.** ish bin äm fēr'ōōntsväntsigstən ougōōst' noin'tsänhōōndərt... gəbō'rən.
On the 4th of *this/next* month.	**Am 4. *dieses/nächsten* Monats.** äm fēr'tən *dē'zəs/nä̱sh'stən* mō'näts.
On April 1st of *this/next* year.	**Am 1. April *dieses/nächsten* Jahres.** äm ār'stən äpril' *dē'zəs/nä̱sh'stən* yä'rəs.
We're leaving on the 20th of August.	**Wir reisen am 20. August ab.** vēr rī'zən äm tsvän'tsish·stən ougōōst' äp.

10

233

| We arrived on the 25th of July. | **Wir sind am 25. Juli angekommen.** vēr zint äm fĭnf'ōōntsväntsish·stən yōō'lē än'gəkōmən. |
| The letter was mailed on the 9th of June. | **Der Brief wurde am 9. Juni abge- schickt.** där brēf vōōr'də äm noin'tən yōō'nē äp'gəshikt. |

Days of the Week

Monday	**der Montag** där mōn'täk
Tuesday	**der Dienstag** där dēn'stäk
Wednesday	**der Mittwoch** där mit'vôh
Thursday	**der Donnerstag** där dôn'ərstäk
Friday	**der Freitag** där frī'täk
Saturday	**der Samstag/Sonnabend** där zäms'täk, där zôn'äbənt
Sunday	**der Sonntag** där zôn'täk

Months

January	**der Januar** där yän'ōō·är
February	**der Februar** där fā'brōō·är
March	**der März** där merts
April	**der April** där äpril'
May	**der Mai** där mī
June	**der Juni** där yōō'nē

234

July	**der Juli** dār yōō'lē
August	**der August** dār ougōōst'
September	**der September** dār zeptem'bər
October	**der Oktober** dār ôktō'bər
November	**der November** dār nōvem'bər
December	**der Dezember** dār dātsem'bər

THE WEATHER

| What's the weather going to be like today? | **Wie wird das Wetter heute?** vē virt däs vet'ər hoi'tə? |
| Have you heard the weather report yet? | **Haben Sie schon den Wetterbericht gehört?** hä'bən zē shōn dān vet'ərberi<u>sh</u>t gəhært'? |

It's going to be ...	**Es wird ...** es virt ...
warm.	**warm.** värm
hot.	**heiß.** hīs
cold.	**kalt.** kä̲lt
cool.	**kühl.** kē̲l
humid.	**schwül.** shvē̲l

| It's going to rain. | **Es wird Regen geben.** es virt rā'gən gā'bən. |

10

235

It's pretty *windy/* *stormy.*	**Es ist ziemlich *windig/stürmisch.***
	es ist tsēm'lish vin'dish/shtēr'mish.

The sky's *clear/* *cloudy.*	**Der Himmel ist *klar/bewölkt.***
	dār him'əl ist klär/bəvelkt'.

What's the temperature?	**Wie viel Grad haben wir?**
	vē fēl grät hä'bən vēr?

It's ... degrees *above/* *below* zero.	**Es sind ... Grad *über/unter* Null.**
	es zint ... grät ē'bər/ōōn'tər nōōl.

INFO Temperatures are generally given in Celsius (Centigrade). Celsius can be converted to Fahrenheit using this formula: (9/5°C)+32 and Fahrenheit to Celsius: (°F-32)·5/9

Here are some approximations:

Fahrenheit	Celsius
104°	40°
86°	30°
68°	20°
50°	10°
32°	0°
14°	–10°
0°	–17,8°

236

air	**die Luft** dē lōōft	
barometric pressure	**der Luftdruck** dār lōōf'drŏŏk	
blizzard	**der Schneesturm** dār shnā'shtŏŏrm	
breeze	**der Luftzug** dār lōōf'tsōōk	
bright	**heiter** hī'tər	
clear	**klar** klär	
climate	**das Klima** däs klē'mä	
cloud	**die Wolke** dē vôl'kə	
cloudburst	**der Wolkenbruch** dār vôl'kənbrōōh	
cold	**kalt** kält	
cool	**kühl** kēl	
damp	**feucht** foisht	
dawn	**die Morgendämmerung** dē môr'gən-dem`ərōōng	
degree	**der Grad** dār grät	
depression	**das Tief** däs tēf	
drizzle	**der Nieselregen** dār nē'zəlrāgən	
dry	**trocken** trôk'ən	
dusk	**die Abenddämmerung** dē ä'bənt-demərōōng	
easterly wind	**der Ostwind** dār ôst'vint	
fog	**der Nebel** dār nā'bəl	
frost	**der Frost** dār frôst	
hail	**der Hagel** dār hä'gəl	

10

hazy	**diesig** dē′zi<u>sh</u>
heat	**die Hitze** dē hit′sə
heatwave	**die Hitzewelle** dē hit′səvelə
high-pressure area	**das Hoch** d<u>a</u>s hō<u>h</u>
hot	**heiß** hīs
humid	**schwül** shv<u>ē</u>l
hurricane	**der Orkan** dār ôrkän′
it's freezing	**es friert** es frērt
it's hailing	**es hagelt** es hä′gəlt
it's lightning	**es blitzt** es blitzt
it's raining	**es regnet** es rāg′nət
it's snowing	**es schneit** es shnīt
it's thawing	**es taut** es tout
it's thundering	**es donnert** es dôn′ərt
lightning	**der Blitz** dār blits
low-pressure area	**das Tief** d<u>a</u>s tēf
moon	**der Mond** dār mōnt
north wind	**der Nordwind** dār nôrt′vint
overcast	**bewölkt** bəv<u>e</u>lkt′
rain	**der Regen** dār rā′gən
rainfall	**die Niederschläge** *(plural)* dē nē′dərshlāgə
shower	**der Regenschauer** dār rā′gənshou·ər
snow	**der Schnee** dār shnā
snow storm	**der Schneesturm** dār shnā′shtoͦorm
southerly wind	**der Südwind** dār z<u>ē</u>t′vint

238

star	**der Stern** dār shtern	
starry sky	**der sternenklare Himmel** dār shter'nənklärə him'əl	
storm	**der Sturm** dār shtŏŏrm	
stormy	**stürmisch** shtēr'mish	
sun	**die Sonne** dē zôn'ə	
sunny	**sonnig** zôn'i<u>sh</u>	
sunrise	**der Sonnenaufgang** dār zôn'ənouf gäng	
sunset	**der Sonnenuntergang** dār zôn'ənōōn'tərgäng	
temperature	**die Temperatur** dē tempərätōōr'	
thaw	**das Tauwetter** däs tou'vetər	
thunder	**der Donner** dār dôn'ər	
thunderstorm	**das Gewitter** däs gəvit'ər	
tornado	**der Tornado** dār tôrnä'dō	
variable	**wechselhaft** vek'səlhäft	
warm	**warm** värm	
weather	**das Wetter** däs vet'ər	
weather report	**der Wetterbericht** dār vet'ərbəri<u>sh</u>t	
west wind	**der Westwind** dār vest'vint	
wet	**nass** n<u>ä</u>s	
wind	**der Wind** dār vint	
wind force	**die Windstärke** dē vint'shterkə	
windy	**windig** vin'di<u>sh</u>	

10

Grammar

ARTICLES

Definite and Indefinite Articles

| | Singular | | |
	Masculine	Feminine	Neuter
Def. Article	**der Mann** the man	**die Frau** the woman	**das Kind** the child
	Plural		
	die Männer the men	**die Frauen** the women	**die Kinder** the children
Indef. Article	**ein Mann** a man	**eine Frau** a woman	**ein Kind** a child

NOUNS

Guide to Gender

Nouns ending in **-er**, especially those denoting a male occupation (**der Kellner**, the waiter), are usually masculine. Words ending in **-chen**, **-lein**, and **-um** are neuter, e.g.: **das Mädchen**, the girl; **das Büchlein**, the booklet; **das Publikum**, the audience.

Words ending in **-in**, **-heit**, **-keit**, **-ung**, and **-e** are usually feminine, e.g.: **die Kellnerin**, the waitress; **die Mehrheit**, the majority; **die Freundlichkeit**, the friendliness; **die Kleidung**, the clothes; **die Sonne**, the sun; **die Tasche**, the purse.

In compound nouns the gender of the last noun is decisive, e.g.:
das Buch, the book, but **die Buchhandlung**, the bookstore.

Declension

Both nouns and articles are declined according to their function in
a sentence. There are four cases: nominative (subject), accusative
(direct object), genitive (possessive case), and dative (indirect
object).

SINGULAR

Nominative	**der Mann**	**die Frau**	**das Kind**
Accusative	**den Mann**	**die Frau**	**das Kind**
Genitive	**des Mann(e)s**	**der Frau**	**des Kind(e)s**
Dative	**dem Mann**	**der Frau**	**dem Kind**

Nominative	**ein Mann**	**eine Frau**	**ein Kind**
Accusative	**einen Mann**	**eine Frau**	**ein Kind**
Genitive	**eines Mann(e)s**	**einer Frau**	**eines Kind(e)s**
Dative	**einem Mann**	**einer Frau**	**einem Kind**

PLURAL

Nominative	**die Männer**	**die Frauen**	**die Kinder**
Accusative	**die Männer**	**die Frauen**	**die Kinder**
Genitive	**der Männer**	**der Frauen**	**der Kinder**
Dative	**den Männern**	**den Frauen**	**den Kindern**

Examples:

Nominative	**Der Mann (die Frau, das Kind) trinkt eine Tasse Tee.** The man (the woman, the child) is drinking a cup of tea.
Accusative	**Ich kann den Mann (die Frau, das Kind) nicht sehen.** I can't see the man (the woman, the child).
Genitive	**Ich kenne den Namen des Mannes (der Frau, des Kindes) nicht.** I don't know the man's (the woman's, the child's) name.
Dative	**Ich gab der Frau (dem Mann, dem Kind) etwas Geld.** I gave the woman (the man, the child) some money.

Plural

Nouns form their plural, in most cases, by adding a suffix (**-n, e, -en,** or **-er**): **die Karte, die Karten; der Helm, die Helme; die Frau, die Frauen; das Kind, die Kinder**. The stem vowel often becomes an umlaut (a → ä: **Mann, Männer**; o → ö: **Sohn, Söhne**; u → ü: **Hut, Hüte**). Sometimes there is no difference in the singular and plural forms except in the definite article, e.g.: **das Brötchen**, the breadroll, **die Brötchen**, the breadrolls; **der Teller**, the plate, **die Teller**, the plates.

PRONOUNS

Personal Pronouns

Nominative		Accusative		Dative	
			Singular		
ich	I	**mich**	me	**mir**	(to) me
du	you *(familiar)*	**dich**	you	**dir**	(to) you
Sie	you *(polite)*	**Sie**	you	**Ihnen**	(to) you
er	he	**ihn**	him	**ihm**	(to) him
sie	she	**sie**	her	**ihr**	(to) her
es	it	**es**	it	**ihm**	(to) it
			Plural		
wir	we	**uns**	us	**uns**	(to) us
ihr	you *(familiar)*	**euch**	you	**euch**	(to) you
Sie	you *(polite)*	**Sie**	you	**Ihnen**	(to) you
sie	they	**sie**	them	**ihnen**	(to) them

Interrogative Pronouns

The singular and plural forms are the same:

Nom.	**wer?**	who?	**was?**	what?
Acc.	**wen?**	who(m)?	**was?**	what?
Gen.	**wessen?**	whose?		
Dat.	**wem?**	(to) who(m)?		

Reflexive Pronouns

Some verbs are reflexive in German. This means they contain a reflexive pronoun (**sich** in the infinitive form: **sich waschen**, to wash oneself; **sich amüsieren**, to have a good time, to enjoy oneself etc.). These pronouns are declined as follows:

Singular		Plural	
mich	myself	**uns**	ourselves
dich	yourself (*familiar*)	**euch**	yourselves (*familiar*)
sich	yourself (*polite*)	**sich**	yourselves (*polite*)
sich	himself, herself, itself, oneself	**sich**	themselves

Examples:

<u>Sie</u> wäscht <u>sich</u> gerade.	She's just getting washed.
<u>Wir</u> haben <u>uns</u> sehr amüsiert.	We had a great time.
<u>Ich</u> muss <u>mich</u> hinlegen.	I have to lie down.

Some reflexive verbs take the dative form of the reflexive pronoun. In the dative myself is **mir** and yourself is **dir**. All the other forms remain the same:

sich (etwas) überlegen	to consider, to think about
Ich werde es mir überlegen.	I'll think about it.
Du wirst es dir überlegen.	You'll think about it.
Sie wird es sich überlegen.	She'll think about it.

ADJECTIVES AND ADVERBS

Adjectives

Adjectives are declined differently according to whether they are used with the definite or the indefinite article:

	Masculine	Feminine	Neuter
		Singular	
Nom.	der junge Mann *the young man*	die nette Frau *the nice woman*	das kranke Kind *the sick child*
Acc.	den jungen Mann	die nette Frau	das kranke Kind
Gen.	des jungen Mannes	der netten Frau	des kranken Kindes
Dat.	dem jungen Mann	der netten Frau	dem kranken Kind
		Plural	
Nom.	die jungen Männer	die netten Frauen	die kranken Kinder
Acc.	die jungen Männer	die netten Frauen	die kranken Kinder
Gen.	der jungen Männer	der netten Frauen	der kranken Kinder
Dat.	den jungen Männern	den netten Frauen	den kranken Kindern
Nom.	ein junger Mann *a young man*	eine nette Frau *a nice woman*	ein krankes Kind *a sick child*
Acc.	einen jungen Mann	eine nette Frau	ein krankes Kind
Gen.	eines jungen Mannes	einer netten Frau	eines kranken Kindes
Dat.	einem jungen Mann	einer netten Frau	einem kranken Kind

Possessive Adjectives

Masculine		Feminine Singular	Neuter
mein	my	**meine**	**mein**
dein	your *(familiar)*	**deine**	**dein**
Ihr	your *(polite)*	**Ihre**	**Ihr**
sein	his, its	**seine**	**sein**
ihr	her	**ihre**	**ihr**
		Plural	
unser	our	**unsere**	**unser**
euer	your *(familiar)*	**eure**	**euer**
Ihr	your *(polite)*	**Ihre**	**Ihr**
ihr	their	**ihre**	**ihr**

These are declined in the same way as the indefinite article **ein(e)** (see previous table) and agree in gender with the noun they qualify:

Er hält seinen wehen Kopf.	He is holding his sore head.
Sie ist meine Schwester.	She's my sister.
Ihre Schuhe sind nass.	Your shoes are wet.

The Comparative and the Superlative

To form the comparative of an adjective add **-er** to the simple form and then add on the adjective endings, e.g.:

schnell → **schneller** + ending, faster; **schön** → **schöner** + ending, nicer, prettier

Ich nahm den schnelleren Aufzug.	I took the faster elevator.
Sie kaufte sich ein schöneres Kleid.	She bought a nicer dress for herself.

Some adjectives change the stem vowel into an umlaut and a few are completely irregular in the comparative:

alt → **älter**, older/elder; **groß** → **größer**, bigger; **gut** →**besser**, better.

To form the superlative of adjectives add **-(e)st** to the simple form of the adjective and then add on the adjective endings, e.g.:

langsam	slow → **langsamer**	slower → **der/die/das langsamste ...** the slowest ...
klein	small → **kleiner**	smaller → **der/die/das kleinste ...** the smallest ...

Adverbs

Adverbs generally have the same ~~form~~ as their corresponding adjectives. The comparative of adverbs takes the same pattern as for adjectives:

laut loud → **lauter** louder, more loudly

The superlative of adverbs is generally formed by adding **-(e)sten** to the simple form of the adverb and inserting **am** before it:

schnell fast → **schneller** faster → **am schnellsten** fastest
Er fährt schnell, aber sie fährt am schnellsten.
He drives fast but she drives the fastest.
Exception: **gut** well → **besser** better → **am besten** best

PREPOSITIONS

In German prepositions determine the case of the noun following or preceding them. Certain combinations of prepositions and articles can be contracted, e.g.: **an dem → am, auf das → aufs, zu der → zur, zu dem → zum** etc.

Prepositions taking the dative case:
aus from, out of / **bei** at; near / **mit** with / **nach** to; after / **seit** since / **von** from / **zu** to / **außer** except; besides / **gegenüber** opposite

Prepositions taking the accusative case:

bis till, until; as far as / **durch** through; by means of / **für** for / **gegen** against / **ohne** without / **um** around, round

Prepositions which can take either the dative or the accusative: **an** on, at; onto, to / **auf** on; onto / **hinter** behind; after; beyond / **in** in; into / **neben** beside, next to / **über** over, above; across / **unter** under, below; among / **vor** in front of; before / **zwischen** between; among

These prepositions take the accusative when expressing movement towards something and the dative when they denote a stationary condition, e.g.: **Er steckte den Ball in seine** (*accusative*) **Tasche**. He put the ball into his bag. But: **Der Ball lag in der** (*dative*) **Tasche.** The ball was in the bag.

VERBS

In German there are two conjugations. The "strong conjugation" (like irregular English verbs) and the "weak conjugation" (regular verbs). Verbs of the strong conjugation have vowel changes in the present tense and irregular past participles and past tenses, e.g.:

essen to eat

ich esse, du isst, Sie essen, er/sie/es isst, wir essen, ihr esst, sie essen;

ich aß I ate;

ich habe ... gegessen I have eaten

fahren to travel/drive

ich fahre, du fährst, Sie fahren, er/sie/es fährt, wir fahren, ihr fahrt, sie fahren;

ich fuhr I traveled/drove

ich bin ... gefahren I have traveled, driven

lesen to read

ich lese, du liest, Sie lesen, er/sie/es liest, wir lesen, ihr lest, sie lesen;

ich las I read (past tense)

ich habe ... gelesen I have read

We have added an ellipsis when giving compound German tenses as this shows you where the tense formation is separated when the past participle or the infinitive is placed at the end of the sentence construction, e.g.:

er hat ... gegeben	he has given/he gave
Er hat mir das Geld gegeben.	He gave me the money.
wir werden ... gehen	we will go
Wir werden später ins Kino gehen.	We'll go to the movies later.

Auxiliary Verbs

In German the auxiliary verbs **haben** to have, **sein** to be, and **werden** to become are used to form compound tenses like the perfect, the pluperfect, the future and the conditional. They are conjugated as follows:

Present tense

haben to have

ich habe	I have/am having	**wir haben**	we have/are having
du hast/ Sie haben	you have/are having	**ihr habt**	you have/are having
er/sie/es hat	he/she/it has/is	**sie haben**	they have/are having

Present tense:

sein to be

ich bin	I am/am being	**wir sind**	we are/are being
du bist/ Sie sind	you are/are being	**ihr seid**	you are/are being
er/sie/es ist	he/she/it is/is being	**sie sind**	they are/are being

werden to become

ich werde	I become/am becoming	wir werden	we become/ are becoming
du wirst/ Sie werden	you become/are becoming	ihr werdet	you become/ are becoming
er/sie/es wird	he/she/it becomes/is becoming	sie werden	they become/ are becoming

Imperfect

ich hatte	I had	ich war	I was	ich wurde	I became
du hattest/		du warst/		du wurdest/	
Sie hatten		Sie waren		Sie wurden	
er/sie/es		er/sie/es		er/sie/es	
hatte		war		wurde	
wir hatten		wir waren		wir wurden	
ihr hattet		ihr wart		ihr wurdet	
sie hatten		sie waren		sie wurden	

The perfect tense is formed with the present tense of the verbs **sein** and **haben** + the past participle (in regular verbs this is formed by removing the **-en** from the infinitive and adding **-t** to the end and **ge-** to the start of the word, e.g.: **kaufen**, to buy, **gekauft**, bought; **sagen**, to say, **gesagt**, said etc.). Some verbs of

26	**sechsundzwanzig** zeks'ōōntsvän'tsi<u>sh</u>
27	**siebenundzwanzig** zē'bənōōntsvän'tsi<u>sh</u>
28	**achtundzwanzig** <u>äh</u>t'ōōntsvän'tsi<u>sh</u>
29	**neunundzwanzig** noin'ōōntsvän'tsi<u>sh</u>
30	**dreißig** drī'si<u>sh</u>
40	**vierzig** fir'tsi<u>sh</u>
50	**fünfzig** finf'tsi<u>sh</u>
60	**sechzig** ze<u>sh</u>'tsi<u>sh</u>
70	**siebzig** zēp'tsi<u>sh</u>
80	**achtzig** <u>äh</u>'tsi<u>sh</u>
90	**neunzig** noin'tsi<u>sh</u>
100	**hundert** hōōn'dərt
101	**hunderteins** hōōndərtīns'
200	**zweihundert** tsvī'hōōndərt
1000	**tausend** tou'zənt
2000	**zweitausend** tvsī'touzənt
10000	**zehntausend** tsān'touzənt

Ordinal Numbers

1.	**erste(r)** ers'tə(r)
2.	**zweite(r)** tsvī'tə(r)
3.	**dritte(r)** drit'ə(r)
4.	**vierte(r)** fēr'tə(r)
5.	**fünfte(r)** finf'tə(r)
6.	**sechste(r)** zeks'tə(r)
7.	**siebte(r)** zēp'tə(r)
8.	**achte(r)** <u>äh</u>'tə(r)
9.	**neunte(r)** noin'tə(r)
10.	**zehnte(r)** tsān'tə(r)

NUMBERS

Cardinal Numbers

0	**null**	nōōl
1	**eins**	īns
2	**zwei**	tsvī
3	**drei**	drī
4	**vier**	fēr
5	**fünf**	fĭnf
6	**sechs**	zeks
7	**sieben**	zē′bən
8	**acht**	̮äht
9	**neun**	noin
10	**zehn**	tsān
11	**elf**	elf
12	**zwölf**	tsv̮elf
13	**dreizehn**	drī′tsān
14	**vierzehn**	fir′tsān
15	**fünfzehn**	fĭnf′tsān
16	**sechzehn**	ze̮sh′tsān
17	**siebzehn**	zēp′tsān
18	**achtzehn**	̮äh′tsān
19	**neunzehn**	noin′tsān
20	**zwanzig**	tsv̮än′tsi̮sh
21	**einundzwanzig**	īn′ōōntsv̮än′tsi̮sh
22	**zweiundzwanzig**	tsvī′ōōntsv̮än′tsi̮sh
23	**dreiundzwanzig**	drī′ōōntsv̮än′tsi̮sh
24	**vierundzwanzig**	fēr′ōōntsv̮än′tsi̮sh
25	**fünfundzwanzig**	fĭnf′ōōntsv̮än′tsi̮sh

Future

The future tense is formed with the present tense of **werden** + the infinitive:

ich werde ... gehen	I will go
du wirst ... bleiben	you will stay
er wird ... kaufen	he will buy
sie wird ... sein	she will be etc.

Conditional

The conditional tense is formed as follows:

ich würde	etc. + the infinitive, e.g.:
ich würde ... essen	I would eat
du würdest ... gehen	you would go
Sie würden lachen	you would laugh
er/sie/es würde ... haben	he/she/it would have
wir würden ... sein	we would be
ihr würdet ... bleiben	you would stay
sie würden ... lachen	they would laugh

motion and a few others use **sein** to form the perfect tense (**gehen, laufen, springen, fahren, sterben, sein, erscheinen** etc.) but most use **haben**:

Ich habe ... gehabt	I have had/I had
du hast ... gehabt	you have had/you had etc.
ich habe ... gewollt	I have wanted/I wanted
du hast ... gewollt	you have wanted/you wanted etc.
ich bin ... gewesen	I have been/I was
du bist ... gewesen	you have been/you were etc.
ich bin ... gefahren	I have traveled/I traveled
du bist ... gefahren	you have traveled/you traveled etc.

Pluperfect

The pluperfect tense is formed with the imperfect tense of **haben** (or **sein** for certain verbs of motion and **sein** itself) + the past participle:

ich hatte ... gehabt	I had had
du hattest ... gehabt	you had had etc.
ich war ... gewesen	I had been
du warst ... gewesen	you had been etc.
ich hatte ... gemacht	I had done
sie hatten ... gehofft	they had hoped
wir waren ... gegangen	we had gone etc.